YOU
Can Find a
FORTUNE

JEANNE HORN

**A FINDER'S GUIDE TO
Some of the World's Missing
Treasures—Large and Small**

BELL PUBLISHING COMPANY • NEW YORK

ACKNOWLEDGMENTS

I wish to thank all the wonderful people who helped make this book possible. I would like to say "thank you" to each one of them individually, but space will not allow it, and so I can mention only a very few.

I would especially like to thank: John Walker, director, National Gallery of Art, Smithsonian Institution; A. Kenneth Snowman, Wartski's Jewelers, London; C. A. Palmer, Insurance Company of North America Companies; R. Gerald McMurtry, director, the Lincoln National Life Foundation; and Gordon Harmer, president, Harmer, Rooke and Company, Inc.

I would also like to thank: Giles E. Dawson, curator of Books and Manuscripts, Folger Shakespeare library; John I. Hennessy, expert on the Black Virgins of Kazan; Loys Malmgren, Public Relations Department, N. W. Ayer and Son; Phyllis Mott, rare book expert; Wayne Nelson, expert on antique radios and television sets; Robert T. Orr, curator, California Academy of Sciences; Rev. Adam J. Otterbein, C.Ss.R., president, Holy Shroud Guild; and Karl F. Wede, of Wede's Nautical Antique Shop, Saugerties, New York.

Library of Congress Catalog Card Number 66-13835

Printed in the United States of America

This edition published by Bell Publishing Company, Inc.,
a division of Crown Publishers, Inc.,
by arrangement with Arco Publishing Co., Inc.

a b c d e f g h

CONTENTS

I   ANYBODY CAN FIND ANYTHING, ANYWHERE
    the what, where, when and how of treasure hunting   7

II   THE EASTER EGG TREASURE
    the lost art works of Fabergé   16

III   LINCOLNIANA
    items that belonged to Abraham Lincoln   20

IV   THE MILLION-DOLLAR AUTOGRAPH AND OTHERS
    autographs, letters and documents   27

V   THE OVERWEIGHT DIAMOND
    fabulous lost gems   33

VI   TREASURE BEYOND PRICE
    the Shroud of Turin   39

VII   SILVER ON THE C SCALE
    musical instruments and lost scores   45

VIII   THE FIVE-MILLION-DOLLAR SKULL
    relics of famous dead   51

IX   THE GIANT AND THE LADY
    the arms of the Venus de Milo   57

X   THE MASTER'S TOUCH
    paintings by the masters   61

XI   TREASURE IN THE TRUNK
    advertisements and artifacts of yesteryear   67

XII   THE GREATEST TREASURE OF THEM ALL
    the story of the Holy Grail   71

XIII   TREASURE IN THE JUNKYARD
    carriages, coaches and cars   74

XIV   THEY WENT THAT-A-WAY
    mementoes of the Old West   79

XV   MISSING PAINTINGS AND A DISAPPEARING ARTIST
    lost works of American artists   83

XVI   FOR THE GLORY OF GOD
    religious treasures   88

XVII   WHODUNIT?
    clues to famous mysteries   93

XVIII THE CHILDREN'S HOUR
childhood treasures 100

XIX MONEY, MONEY EVERYWHERE
nickels, half-dollars and dollars 106

XX THE GOLDEN HORSESHOES
lost treasures of the Crusaders 109

XXI PAGES AND PAGES OF GOLD
rare and valuable editions 112

XXII PRINTS EXTRAORDINAIRE
old prints and photographs 121

XXIII GOLD DUST IN A BALL OF WAX
carvings, cigar-store Indians, hitching posts, barbers' poles 126

XXIV GLASS AND MORE GLASS
Venetian to Stiegel 130

XXV MISCELLANEA
clothing, clocks and bells 137

XXVI FURNITURE
Chippendale to Franklin 141

XXVII DIAMONDS ALL AROUND YOU
where to look for them 146

XXVIII FOUR-ALARM TREASURE
fire marks of yesteryear 151

XXIX DEAD WHALES, HAIR NETS—AND A DASH OF BEAUTY
women's follies through the ages 158

XXX EAT, DRINK AND BE MERRY
china, silver, spoons 164

XXXI PAPER FORTUNES
rare stamps 168

XXXII ANYTHING THAT GLITTERS
topaz, amber, pearls, gold, emeralds and jade 175

XXXIII RAZZ-MA-TAZZ
campaign memorabilia 180

XXXIV THE BLACK VIRGINS OF KAZAN
the miracle icons of Russia 187

XXXV CANDLESTICK ROCK IS MISSING
mementoes of sports and games 191

XXXVI SUNKEN AND BURIED TREASURE
treasure in the earth and under the sea 195

BIBLIOGRAPHY 200

INDEX 206

I

ANYBODY CAN FIND ANYTHING, ANYWHERE

The What, Where, When and How of
Treasure Hunting

MANY years ago, in Maryland, a man was killed for his gold; then, as in most treasure stories, the thieves for one reason or another buried the gold. Today, so the legend goes, the treasure is guarded by the ghost of a blue dog, who remained loyal even after death.

The ghost of the blue dog does not guard all treasure, however—for in truth, anyone can find treasure, anywhere, any time.

Did you know that there is a missing diamond that weighs one and one third pounds? That an autograph of William Shakespeare's could be worth a million dollars? That the Black Prince's ruby might not be among the crown jewels of England after all?

Did you know that the largest painting in the world is missing? That the skull of Mkwawa is lost? That a piece of the Holy Shroud of Turin was given away as a present? That George Washington's carriage was broken up and the pieces given away as souvenirs?

Or had you forgotten that the Venus de Milo may soon have her arms again? That one hundred and sixteen pages of the Book of Mormon are missing? That there is a man who goes around finding people to give money to? That there is a two-hundred-thousand-dollar dream car at the bottom of the ocean? That there are missing paintings, pieces of the Colossus of Rhodes, gems, mines, furniture, golden horseshoes, autographs, musical instruments, automobiles, books, radios and television sets, items of clothing, Arthur Godfrey memorabilia, saloon signs, baseballs and false teeth?

WHAT is treasure? It can be anything!
   It can be a foot-bath! The Queen of France, Marie Antoinette, rested her feet by dipping them in a hand-painted tin foot-bath. Not too long ago, in Paris, that same foot-bath had a price tag of four thousand dollars on it.

   Treasure can be butter, if you live at a certain time and place. It is said that in ancient Ireland butter was reckoned as wealth.

   It can be a needle! There is a so-called needle room in a building in Kent, where, in the time of Cromwell, four women of the Culpeper family did their fancy needlework. Until 1901, the needle room was as it had been during the time of Cromwell. Even one of the needles that had been used by one of the Culpeper women was still sticking in the cloth, just as she had left it. But when a party of sightseers was allowed to pass through the room the temptation became too great, and the needle disappeared.

   Or money in a suitcase! An old woman was reported missing. Months later, workmen found a battered old suitcase in her home. It contained one hundred and sixty thousand dollars.

   A fresco! An overhead fresco dating from the Renaissance was discovered at Oxford when a ceiling collapsed because a frozen water pipe had burst!

   A Great Seal! According to the National Geographic Society, Maryland's Great Seal disappeared during the lifetime of Lord Baltimore, at a time when he was out of power.

   A record of the dead! Between October 6 and 29, 1944, a record was kept in Hebrew of the prisoners who were put to death in the gas chambers at Auschwitz. The records, thirty-eight pages of names, were put in a glass pot. Not too long ago, this pot was found, very close to the site of a crematory at the same concentration camp.

   Papers dropped from a balloon! When Louis XVI and his wife

Marie Antoinette were returned to Paris after their unsuccessful attempt to escape their fate, the people were so exuberant that a celebration ensued. One feature of this celebration was the dropping from a balloon of numerous copies of the Constitution.

Wallpaper! In Maryland, an antique lover spotted some fine old wallpaper. He paid fifty dollars for it, then went about the laborious task of removing the dirt without damaging the paper. The National Society of Interior Designers bought it from him for two thousand, five hundred dollars. Today, that wallpaper, donated by the Society hangs in the diplomatic reception room of the White House!

A book! Herb Caen, columnist for the *San Francisco Chronicle,* tells about first editions of J. D. Salinger's *Catcher in the Rye.* Sold originally for three dollars apiece, the first-edition copies now bring anywhere from fifty to one hundred and fifty dollars.

A tombstone! A historic tombstone has been stolen out of one of California's state parks.

A land deed! A deed for the land that eventually became a portion of the city of Detroit, Michigan, sold for over three thousand dollars at a recent Parke-Bernet auction. It was the original deed from one of the Indian nations.

Even a ball of mud can be worth something—if it's from the Midwest, and if it's fossilized!

Or a butterfly on the wing can be treasure. Back in the late 1800's, the Baron Rothschild thought nothing of paying two thousand, five hundred dollars for a butterfly. There are certain kinds of butterflies of which only one known specimen has ever been caught. There are other kinds of butterflies of which there are only two or three known examples in existence—other than those still flying free in the air. Butterflies of rare types would be worth a great deal of money.

Who can find treasure? Anyone!

A shopper! A woman bought some picture frames for five dollars. One of the frames held an early Sargent.

A servant! A woman left a cupboard full of odds and ends to one of her servants. These odds and ends turned out to include some miniatures that were worth two thousand pounds.

Anyone at all!

When can you find treasure? Any time, no matter what you are doing!

A little girl, playing hide and seek with her brother, found a jar of gold coins dating back to before the year 1000 A.D.

While going through the papers of a dead relative, a couple came across documents giving clues to the burial of cans full of money near the home of the deceased. They haven't found the cans full of money yet, but they're still looking.

A man was leveling out the lot next to his home. He noticed a tin can sticking out of the ground, which proved to contain gold coins.

Where can you find treasure? Anywhere at all!

Around old buildings! A workman on a demolition project, in an area where they were clearing away old buildings, dug up a valuable old theatre handbill.

In old clothes! A copy of a ballad written by Benjamin Franklin, no copy of which had been located in almost two hundred years, was found in the pocket of an old leather jacket. Another old jacket, given to the Salvation Army, was found to contain four thousand dollars hidden in its lining.

In sidewalks! Four live cannon balls and one dud were gingerly removed from a sidewalk in Houston, Texas!

In scrap heaps! An antique dictaphone was recently salvaged from a scrap heap.

In fireplaces! Sixty dollars in gold was found in the ruins of an old fireplace.

In attics! In 1953, notes made by William Clark, the famous explorer and partner of Meriwether Lewis, turned up in an attic. Along with the notes made during his explorations were maps drawn by Clark himself.

In walls! In the parts of America where the Revolutionary War was fought, cannon balls can still be found lodged in walls.

In the city dumps! An old album, given away by one of California's early Spanish settlers, was found in a city dump. It is now in a museum.

Anywhere at all! Venetian jewelry dating back to the sixteenth century was found in, of all places, Mashonaland, Southern Rhodesia, at a time when that part of South Africa had just been opened to the outside world. How did it get there? Who knows?

Try second-hand stores, rummage sales, auctions, antique shops. Go through your grandmother's attic, if she'll let you, but first make sure she hasn't also read this book, because, if she has, she'll be going through it herself.

What do you do with what you find? Well, first of all, do not rely on your own experience. Sometimes it is worth the price of a good appraisal to find out what you have. In the meantime, museums, libraries and antique dealers will be able to help you.

If you don't live close to a museum or a dealer, write to them. Send a complete description of the object—include a drawing, a copy of a hallmark, a rubbing of a coin. On larger items, send a *complete* description. If possible, enclose a photograph of the object or a photostatic copy of the document.

Remember that museums do not make evaluations. They will not tell you the monetary value of the item you have, but they can help you determine its age and authenticity, which is after all what you need to be able to sell what you have.

Then, too, a museum may decide it wants to see the item. If you must ship it to a museum, wrap it carefully, register it and insure it.

Sometimes, of course, even the experts make mistakes! Never give up at the first opinion, even if it sounds favorable. The next one might be better.

A ND *always* check before you jump to conclusions! The name "Stradivarius," for example, sends scores of treasure hunters flocking into the junk stores and the attics whenever they hear it. The mere idea of a new Strad having been found is enough to reinforce forever their belief that treasures can indeed be found.

Recently, in Wales, a recluse died. Authorities went through his belongings, remembering, as they did so, the stories the old man had been wont to tell—stories of fabulous violins that he owned. No one had believed him, yet some did remember having heard faint strains of violin music emanating from his house at odd hours of the night.

They found the violins, all right. As a matter of fact, they found four violins that American newspapers later wrote up as possible Strads. When I contacted M. C. Whitelock, Clerk to the Council, Narberth, Pembrokeshire, Wales, he wrote in reply: "I have made enquiries and have ascertained that so far as is known none of the numerous violins owned by the late Hermann Idle of Narbeth were made by Stradivarius."

It was too bad, but the point is that the violins were evidently not made by Stradivarius. Newsmen jumped too soon at the possibility that they might have been.

Sometimes, however, such faith *can* be justified! It was justified in the case of Arpad d'Zurko of San Francisco, California, who bought an old violin in a shop in that city. The violin had a Stradivarius label, but it could have been a copy, of which there are many.

In this case, the dealer was ready to discount the label, as he had seen many violins with fake Strad labels pasted on the inside. As a matter of fact, he told D'Zurko that he should disregard the label completely. He said that he thought the violin had been made by one Carlo Landolfi, who did, it is true, make good violins. But there is as much difference between a good violin and a real Strad as there is between a rhinestone and a diamond.

D'Zurko listened to the dealer, respecting his opinion; but the violin had become something special to him. Whether it was because of his university education and highly developed musical ability or because of his gypsy blood, no one will ever really know—but he knew that this violin was no Landolfi!

Referred to as the Gypsy Violinist, D'Zurko was not one of those publicity-seeking "gypsies" who usually turn out to be Boston Irish or even Pennsylvania Dutch. And so, because of his belief in himself and in his violin, he named it the Gypsy Stradivarius. He did this before the violin was authenticated, but D'Zurko had that much faith in his instrument.

Most of the people he came into contact with thought his violin was a fake, a phony, a copy—and you can't really blame them. To find a real Strad is a dream anyone would like have come true, but most so-called finds turn out to be nothing but fakes or copies.

A friend of D'Zurko's, Frank Passa, a San Francisco violin maker, talked D'Zurko into getting an appraisal of the instrument from Rembert Wurlitzer in New York. One of the strangest coincidences in musical history happened at this point. Rembert Wurlitzer had just returned from Cremona, Italy, where he had seen a strange violin mold. The mold was definitely of a Stradivarius type, but Wurlitzer had never seen a Strad made from this particular mold. It puzzled him.

He had been back in New York only a short time, when one day the Gypsy Violin was brought into his office for appraisal. It had been made in the very mold Wurlitzer had seen in Cremona! Wurlitzer issued a certificate of authentication for D'Zurko's violin, believing the instrument to be the work of Francesco Stradivari. He has also stated that the particular model of Strad that D'Zurko owns is rarely seen. According to Wurlitzer, the purfling on the violin is very unusual and has been seen on only one other Stradivarius, a model having been made by Antonio Stradivari.

Today the Gypsy Violin still belongs to Arpad d'Zurko, the Gypsy Violinist, the man who had enough faith in his fiddle to label it a Strad before the experts ever even saw it. This was the one old violin that really did turn out to be a genuine Stradivarius!

How much is what you find worth?

It varies, of course. A price may be quoted, either in this book or elsewhere, and then fall apart at the last moment, either because the supply of the items has increased or because the demand for it has fallen. Either way, the final price depends on the collectors—and how badly they want a given item.

Any item you have will bring only what the market will bear. If you have something the collectors want, they will pay for it. But it depends on both supply and demand. One collector of Remington prints died of hunger rather than quit buying new prints.

Not all the treasures in this book will bring fabulous fortunes. Some of them may not even be worth the effort you put into looking for them, yet they are all worth something, and whoever heard of someone leaving a ten-dollar-bill in the garbage can because it was too much trouble to look around for it?

Many times it is a question of hanging on to what you have until you find the right collector. He must want it badly enough and he must want it *now*. He must want it as badly, perhaps, as the female collector, who, while on a trip through the countryside, spotted a Staffordshire blue platter that she decided she must have at all costs. The owner of the platter, in her turn, greatly admired the skirt the collector was wearing. The collector immediately removed her skirt. She walked off in her underslip, but under her arm she proudly carried the Staffordshire blue platter! She knew what she wanted and got it, regardless of the price she had to pay.

WHATEVER you do, don't get so anxious that you're like the sailor on board a pirate ship anchored off one of the islands, who made the mistake of buying what a native told him was a piece of ambergris. The so-called ambergris turned out, on closer inspection, to be nothing more than hand-molded goat manure.

This man obviously thought that something found in exotic surroundings and purchased under strange circumstances must be treasure. It is a good idea, really, to look for ambergris, but you don't have to sail on a pirate ship or buy from a native to do it! Treasure is usually found closer to home—whether it's a piece of ambergris that floats up on your own beach or a lost piano that had been right under your nose all the time—as was the case with the Siena Pianoforte.

Young Avner Carmi, grandson of pianist Mathis Yanovsky, had heard stories and legends about this fabulous piano all his life. The building of the piano had taken the lifetimes of four generations of artisans to complete. The piano was carved out of wood that had supposedly been part of the pillars of the Temple of Solomon in Jerusalem. Reputed to be unbelievably beautiful, the instrument was intricately carved and embellished with figures of cherubs and the heads of composers.

Carmi had become a piano repairman, and he was still fascinated by the legend of the Siena Pianoforte. He called often at the court of Victor Emmanuel III, hoping to get permission merely to see the piano, which at that time was in the Quirinal in Rome. He was refused each time. During one of these attempts to speak to Victor Emmanuel, he was almost arrested on suspicion of plotting the King's assassination.

During the First World War, Carmi was assigned to the task of salvaging items left behind by the retreating German army under Rommel. One of these objects was the strangest piano Carmi had ever seen. It was found early one morning in the dunes and, because it might have been booby-trapped, minesweepers had been used on it. The piano would not work, Carmi saw, because it was partly filled with sand. Keys were missing, and various other items had been changed or added. The most striking feature, however, was the casing of the piano—the entire instrument had been covered with hard plaster.

Carmi felt that the thing should not be destroyed, because after all it *was* a piano—but it certainly was a far cry from the beautiful Siena

Pianoforte, which he would so much like to find. There was no telling what the retreating Germans had done with the famous instrument.

In any event, Carmi talked the authorities into letting him repair the plaster piano enough so that it could be used, even though it remained in its plaster case. Then, for some time, all over Italy and Sicily, he seemed to see the plaster piano wherever he went, since it was being used by entertainers.

After the war, Carmi went back to his home and his old trade. One of the first things he saw on returning home was the plaster piano, abandoned in the street. This time Carmi refused to see to its repair, because the keys, the pedals, everything seemed to be missing—except, of course the plaster case. He left it sitting in the sun; but the next day something seemed to draw him back to where he had left it, only to find that the piano was gone. He was sure he had seen the last of it.

Yet it wasn't very long after that that a man brought the plaster piano in and asked that Carmi repair it. The man later changed his mind, becoming quite angry about it. He hit the piano violently with his fist as he demanded the return of the down payment he had made to Carmi for the repair bill.

Carmi handed him the money willingly, because he had seen what the force of the man's blow had done to the plaster covering of the piano. The plaster had cracked, and beneath the piece that came loose Carmi was looking at one of the cherubs on the Siena Pianoforte, for which he had looked for so many years. He had found the pianoforte—and it had been right under his nose all the time!

II

THE EASTER EGG TREASURE

The Lost Art Works of Fabergé

E VEN an Easter egg can be worth a fortune—if it was designed by Fabergé, Court Jeweler to the Czar of Russia.

Easter eggs by Fabergé were not just another gift for Easter but very special creations made for the royal family of Russia—and made with such imagination and craftsmanship that the world has never before or since seen their like.

Fabergé was one of the greatest jewelers of his era. His shop in St. Petersburg, Russia, reached a height of fame unknown to other jewelers, even in a day when jewels for royal families were considered necessities for maintaining their prestige and station in life.

In Russia, the royal family was headed for a revolution that would spread across their nation like wild rot—and destroy them in the process. But in the early morning hours of the many Easter Sundays which preceded the chaos of the Revolution, war and bloodshed were not even thought of; and each Easter Sunday was begun with a presentation of the royal eggs.

Each Easter morning the Czar himself presented a royal egg to the Czarina, and an equally beautiful egg was presented to the Dowager Empress. Altogether there were fifty-seven imperial Easter eggs made and presented to the royal family. Today these eggs are valued at $5,000,000.

The exact date the first imperial egg was made is not known, but it was probably in 1884. The eggs were fine and masterful examples of the best art in Russia. The shells were decorated on the outside with pearls, diamonds and rubies. Opening of the shells revealed the eggs' inner secrets: miniature crowns and rings, picture frames, and platinum swans; golden rosebuds and miniature ruby eggs. One of these eggs even held within it a small train, perfect in every detail.

Yet the art of Fabergé was swept along on the tides of the Revolution. When chaos struck, refugees from all walks of life sold everything they could to gather enough money to get away from the attacking horde. What they could not sell and what was not lost, the Soviets claimed for themselves.

A custom begun by Alexander III in an attempt to cheer up his wife, and later continued by Nicholas II—who gave two eggs a year, one to his wife and one to Alexander III's widow—thus ended in Revolution. Fabergé himself was finished in Russia.

His work, however, remains. Most of the imperial eggs have been preserved in collections both in Russia and in England. Yet there are some that are missing. There are four of these fabulous eggs which were lost in the chaos of Revolution—and they have never been found.

THE first of these missing eggs is the Danish Silver Jubilee Egg, which was presented to Marie Feodorovna by Alexander III in the year 1888. Since the egg was made in celebration of the Silver Jubilee of the King of Denmark, its design was in keeping with the occasion.

A white and pale blue egg, encrusted with precious gems, a diamond-set fillet, a diamond monogram and carved golden masks, it is topped with a Danish royal elephant and supported by three of the Danish heraldic lions.

When the egg was opened, it revealed a two-sided portrait screen topped by diamonds, crowns and initials. The screen holds two portraits, one of King Christian of Denmark and one of Queen Louise of Denmark. Approximately ten inches high, this egg is surely one of the most fantastic of the world's missing treasures.

The first egg ever presented to Alexandra Feodorovna is among the missing eggs. Much smaller than the Danish Silver Jubilee Egg, it is only three inches high, made of engraved gold, translucent strawberry reds and opaque white enamels; it sports gold mounts and Cupid's arrows set with rose diamonds. The date of the gift of the egg (1895) is clearly inscribed on the base immediately below a rose diamond. On the top of the egg is a portrait of Nicholas II.

When the egg is opened, the first item you will see will be a golden rosebud; yet, after removing the rosebud from the egg, you will discover another item within the rosebud: an imperial crown of rubies and diamonds. But even then the treasures are not exhausted, for within the crown itself will be found a miniature ruby egg.

Certainly, this second of the lost eggs, known as the "Rosebud Egg," is one of the most beautiful of the missing treasures of the world.

Inside the third missing egg is a platinum swan which, when wound up, wags its tail, moves along a certain course and raises and lowers its head. As a final touch, the wings themselves open and each platinum feather is seen distinctly.

The swan sits on a lake which is nothing less than a single aquamarine. Water lilies, in four colors of gold, decorate the lake as well as the handle which lifts the swan and his lake from the egg. The outside of the golden egg is mat enameled mauve, decorated with a rose diamond trellis, and at the top as well as the bottom of the egg will be found single, large, portrait diamonds.

Presented to Alexandra Feodorovna by Nicholas II in 1906, and only four inches high, this so-called "Swan Egg" is the third and one of the most beautiful of the missing imperial eggs.

The last of the missing eggs is appropriately called the "Egg with Love Trophies," since it contains a miniature picture frame which, in a lovely design of enamel and diamonds, forms a heart.

In keeping with the Love Trophy theme of the egg, the strut of the frame forms the signature NIKI since it was a gift from Nicholas II to Alexandra Feodorovna. It was Nicholas' portrait which was in the heart-shaped frame.

On the top of the outside of the egg is a basket of roses made of rose diamonds, gold, pearls, enamels and rubies. At the base of the egg are four quivers, and peeping out of these are arrow-top set diamonds. The body of the egg is gold enameled with pale blue. The decorations are carved gold and white enamel bands.

The date of the creation of this egg is not known, but it was probably either 1910 or 1911, and only the approximate measurement of the egg is known. It is thought that the entire egg stands nine inches high while the picture frame is approximately three and one half inches high.

Yet, whether the actual measurements are known or not, this egg with its lovely "love trophies" could never be mistaken for anything but what it is: a fortune in the form of one of the most fantastic Easter eggs ever created.

Any of these missing eggs are worth a fortune—if you can find them.

Yet these are not the only things Fabergé made that are missing, including Easter eggs which were smaller than the imperial eggs and which were made for the families of the nobility. These were small, jeweled eggs which were designed to be worn on long chains as necklaces.

Fabergé made many things, all of them exquisite. He made cigarette cases and clocks, and miniature animals and items for milady's dressing table. He made tie pins and cuff links, and crosses—and all of them collectors' items—if you can find one of them.

They would not have, of course, the value of one of the imperial Easter eggs but, certainly, they would be worth a great deal. Anything by Fabergé is worth something—and the imperial eggs are worth the most of all—if you can find them.

But even the lowly, everyday eggshell merely decorated for Easter can be worth a fortune—if you know one when you see it.

Not too many years ago an eggshell was sold for twenty-five thousand gold francs, but it was not just any eggshell. It was a rare egg painted by a master craftsman. There was a time when such artists as Watteau, Lancret and Boucher painted eggshells for Easter. Not always of a religious nature, yet they were gay eggs painted for the Easter season. And today they would be worth a small fortune—if you can find them.

III

LINCOLNIANA

Treasures from the Time of Abraham Lincoln

THERE is a missing letter which is worth $100,000 if you can find it.

On November 21, 1864, the *Boston Transcript* published an appeal to the general public, an appeal which was in the very finest newspaper tradition.

A widow needed help, and the paper was asking the general public to acknowledge her need. In sorrowful terms the *Boston Transcript* told the story of a woman who, before the advent of the war between the states, had had five sons. Now those sons were dead—dead on the field of battle in defense of the Union.

The newspaper cried out for her, begging the people for their sympathy and their help in this, her time of need. Throughout the nation, people read the story and felt sorry for the grieving mother.

One person in particular read the story and felt deep sorrow because of it. This reader wrote a letter to the widow, telling her of his sympathy. In due time the letter was delivered to the widow, and, when she opened it, this is what she read:

Executive Mansion,

Washington, Nov. 21, 1864

To Mrs. Bixby, Boston, Mass.

Dear Madam: I have been shown in the files of the War Department a statement of the Adjutant General of Massachusetts that you are the mother of five sons who have died gloriously on the field of battle.

I feel how weak and fruitless must be any words of mine which should attempt to beguile you for the grief of a loss so overwhelming. But I cannot refrain from tendering to you the consolation that may be found in the thanks of the Republic they died to save.

I pray that our Heavenly Father may assuage the anguish of your bereavement, and leave you only the cherished memory of the loved and lost, and the solemn pride that must be yours, to have laid so costly a sacrifice upon the altar of freedom.

Yours, very sincerely and respectfully,
A. Lincoln

Mrs. Bixby

Today, the original of that letter which the widow opened and read such a long time ago would be worth $100,000—if you could find it.

The ironic part of the whole episode of that letter is that Lincoln had been completely misled in his understanding of the situation. Mrs. Bixby's five sons were *not* killed on the battlefield, although it is true that two of them did die in battle; but there were also two sons who, instead of dying "gloriously on the field of battle," ignominiously deserted their army and their cause. Neither did the fifth son die in battle, yet he, at least, did not desert. Rather, he was honorably discharged.

On November 21, there had been the plea for Mrs. Bixby in the *Boston Transcript*, written by Adjutant General William Schouler. Lincoln had already had information about the widow at the time this item was printed, but on publication of the appeal Lincoln wrote to Schouler for additional details. With all of this, it seems rather amazing that there should have been such a mistake made, although it was certainly not Mr. Lincoln's mistake, but rather the mistakes of those around him.

But the ironic fact that the letter which Lincoln wrote was composed in error certainly does not detract either from the historical, moral or monetary value of the letter. The beauty of the letter will remain forever, and the monetary value of the letter today stands at $100,000. Yet, can you find it?

Where it is now, nobody knows. We do know that Lincoln himself did not mail the letter, because he did not have Mrs. Bixby's address. He gave it to Schouler, who had it delivered.

It would seem then that the letter disappeared almost immediately after Mrs. Bixby received it. Members of her family seemed to feel that she did not have the letter at the time of her death in 1878.

Today no one knows where it could be; but the value of the letter was apparent almost immediately. Facsimiles and forgeries, both, have flooded the country time after time.

As early as 1891, one man with an eye for business, Tobin by name, registered an engraving of the Lincoln letter with the Librarian of Congress on April 25, 1891. He called it "Lincoln's Letter" and sold copies for $2 apiece—in a day when $2 went a lot further than it does today.

Sometimes, today, these old facsimiles are found, and thought, with all honest intentions, by hopeful treasure hunters, to be the original. They are, of course, disappointed to find they have what is only a facsimile. Yet the search continues for the original letter.

The story of this letter is filled with legends like the one that the original of the Bixby letter is in the Library of Congress, but unfortunately (or rather fortunately for the treasure hunter) this is not so.

The original was, also, at one time supposed to be on exhibit at Huber's Museum in New York City—at least according to a copy of said "original" put out by Huber himself.

It has also been reported that the original letter was in the J. Pierpont Morgan collection, but the Morgan family reported that they knew nothing about the letter.

Many, many times it has been said that the Bostonian Society had the original, but the society has denied this emphatically.

The letter may have been destroyed—and if it has been then it is lost to the treasure hunter. Yet, I do not think so. As stated above, many forgeries and many honest facsimiles have been made. Copies of the letter were printed in the daily newspapers less than a week after Mrs. Bixby received the original.

It must be true, then, that somewhere along the line—at a time when the value of the letter was already apparent—that the original was in hands other than the Widow Bixby's. Otherwise where did the copies come from? You must have an original from which to make a copy. Somewhere along the line someone had the original and from that he made the first copies.

With luck, that original letter is still in existence, and you can trade it for $100,000—if you can find it.

IF you can find an autograph copy of the Gettysburg Address, you can almost name your own price for it. One copy known to be authentic sold for $54,000.

This is the speech which is common knowledge to every schoolboy. Any child can begin this famous oration, which begins with "Four score and seven years ago . . ."

The Address, which was given on November 19, 1863, was spoken at the dedication of the battleground of Gettysburg, a national cemetery.

There are known, today, to be in existence five copies of the Gettysburg Address. The five extant papers include Lincoln's first draft, the reading text, and the revised copies made up after the speech had been delivered.

Yet besides these known copies are the stories of yet another copy —a copy which has never been found. This missing version of the speech was an autograph copy which was made up for Judge David Mills and was evidently written the night before the Gettysburg dedication ceremony, since Lincoln stayed at Mills' home as a guest on that night.

No one knows where that copy is now, but if you can find it you can almost name your own price for it—perhaps even as high as the aforementioned $54,000.

Yet there are other things which belonged to Lincoln which today are missing—and which can be of value to the treasure hunter.

The sport of hunting for missing Lincolniana heightens in furor year by year. The admirers of Lincoln increase by the thousands as each year passes, as they seek more information and more facts concerning the man who was probably America's greatest statesman. Accordingly they also increase their desire for the things which he owned, used or touched.

There was a pen which Lincoln allegedly had in his possession on the night he died. Today, no one knows where it is.

Originally, the pen had been one of a pair which had been presented to Lincoln at the time of his inauguration, but the penholders have a far older history than that. In a much earlier time there had been a desk which belonged to the captain of the Mayflower. Later the lid of that desk was made into a carved chest which held surveying instruments, and that chest was presented to George Washington. Then, in turn, the box was made over into the pair of penholders.

Lincoln presented one of these pens to a Mr. Isaac Reed, and he promised Mr. Reed that he would forward to him papers showing the authenticity of the pen—but three days later Lincoln was murdered. The papers had been filled out but were lost in the confusion of Lincoln's death.

Reed treasured his Lincoln pen and took it all over the world with him, asking various people to use it as they signed their autographs for him. One of those who did so, using this famous pen, was Queen Victoria of England.

The other pen was the one which was allegedly in Lincoln's possession the night he died. As to the value of this pen, if it could be found, there is no way of telling, without of course finding it and holding it for auction. At one time, Reed had the opportunity to sell the pen he owned for three hundred English pounds—quite a sum in those days.

Pens, of course, are not the only missing items of Lincoln. Even his watches are cause for diligent search. On many occasions Lincoln was presented with watches, a common form of official and semi-official gift in those days. Not all of these watches have been found—and they are well worth looking for.

Even his hats are items of value, but not in the way it might seem. While it is true that Lincoln hats are collectors' items, it must also be remembered that Lincoln used his famous stovepipe hats for convenient storage places. In these hats he put papers of all kinds— from items relating to his law practice to official state documents. Almost anything, and possibly something of great value, might be found in one of these old hats.

Collectors ask for such items of wearing apparel as boots, socks, gloves, coats, and even his nightgowns. These items of course are not of great value, yet they are worth enough to have them checked by an expert.

Even Lincoln canes, rings and cuff buttons are sought. This Lincolniana frenzy extends even to items belonging to members of the Lincoln family. There is the story of Mrs. Lincoln's garnets—although this is a story which, heard many years ago, this author has been unable to verify.

It is the story of Mrs. Lincoln's need for hard cash and, like many other American women, she sold her jewels to raise some money— in this case a set of garnets.

Although this story may not be true, Mrs. Lincoln did like jewelry. Tiffany's in New York, for example, made for her a matching set of seed-pearl earrings and necklace to be worn at her husband's Second Inaugural.

Tiffany's today no longer has any records of the seed pearls, although, according to Mr. Wm. J. Fielding of Tiffany's, ". . . understand some of the institutions in Washington, D.C. have some of these pieces and photographs of them."

Garnets, powder horns and wallets! The mania for Lincolniana extends even to their furniture. Furniture from both the White House and the Springfield house are sought by collectors, with particular attention given to chairs, since the chairs of the family seem to carry more interest than other items of furniture.

Among the chairs associated with the Lincolns, and which are known to be missing, are a tall, hall chair and a set of plain, wooden chairs which had flowers painted on their backs. Chairs also worth watching for are those which Lincoln used in his law practice, because they seem to have a special appeal to collectors.

The value of a Lincoln chair is difficult to judge, since each item would of necessity be of different condition and make. Also the price of the item would vary according to how much part the chair had played in the history of the nation. For example, a chair which Lincoln had used at the time of a great historic event would be of far more value than just any chair which he had used.

However, I have seen prices ranging from $100 to $250 per chair.

Chairs, hats, canes, or whatever, there is a chance of finding them —all except one item which is probably the strangest of all lost Lincolniana: an entire log cabin.

"Log cabin" is synonymous with the very name of Lincoln, and in 1830 when Lincoln's family moved to Illinois, Abraham pitched in to help clear the land, fence the property, and build the inevitable log cabin.

Years later, in 1865, this cabin was an item of much public interest when it was displayed as an exhibit of the Chicago Sanitary Fair. Following this exhibition, the log cabin was shown at Barnum's Museum in New York City. Eventually the cabin was loaded aboard a ship so that it could be exhibited in England. But the ship was lost at sea, carrying with it a piece of Lincolniana which can never be replaced. Surely, this must be the strangest of the lost Lincolniana.

The more everyday items belonging to Lincoln are, however, quite within the scope of today's treasure hunter, from the very valuable missing autograph copy of the Gettysburg Address to the satchels which he carried. Anything which he owned or used is worth checking—of course, being careful that you have all the proper facts.

Do not, above all, be like the person who tried to sell a piece of rail which he claimed Lincoln had split while he was still living on the family farm in Kentucky. He "forgot" the fact that when the Lincoln family left the Kentucky farm, "Little Abe" was only two years old—and not even Abraham Lincoln rated the title of a two-year-old rail splitter.

But if you have anything at all which belonged to the Lincoln family, have it checked. It is bound to be worth something.

IV

THE MILLION-DOLLAR AUTOGRAPH
AND OTHERS

Autographs, Letters and Documents

A MAN scrawls his name unthinkingly across the bottom of a letter, a valentine or a money order and never realizes that the scrawl may someday be worth a small fortune—depending, of course, on exactly who he was and what it was that he signed.

A group of several letters by astronaut John Glenn cost the lucky buyer four hundred and twenty-five dollars at a recent auction; yet, at the same auction, certain of the Lindbergh papers sold for three thousand, five hundred dollars.

One reason for the discrepancies apparent between the value of the Lindbergh papers and the Glenn items was the fact that the contents were so very different. Lindbergh's papers discussed his flight to Paris, whereas Glenn's letters discussed his automobile. Naturally, the Lindbergh papers would bring more.

The difference between the value of a signature alone and a signature affixed to a letter or handwritten document of historical importance is indicated by the signature of John Hancock, which is worth from fifty dollars to five hundred dollars, depending on whether or not it is merely a signature or whether it is affixed to a letter.

A letter written by Benjamin Franklin discussing his experiments, his political activities or the great events of his time would have a far

27

greater value than, say, a letter that merely stated that it was raining out and that he hoped the weather would turn fine.

A Franklin autograph can be worth from three hundred dollars to three thousand dollars, depending upon the type of document to which it is affixed, the content of the document, and other considerations.

Fame alone, however, can give value to an individual signature. Everyone remembers Barbara Frietchie, who has become a legend because of the poem by John Greenleaf Whittier. Yet, not everyone realizes that a Frietchie autograph is quite rare. As a matter of fact, papers signed by Barbara Frietchie number less than a dozen—by this I mean the number of Frietchie documents which are *known* to exist. How many may be in America's attics, no ones knows. Documents autographed by her have sold for as high as three hundred and sixty dollars.

A historic document complete with Napoleon's signature was recently evaluated at one hundred and forty-five dollars. A signed letter written by Danton, the French revolutionary, was recently evaluated as being worth two hundred dollars.

Diaries of all kinds can be of great importance, especially if they relate to famous or historic personages. One such was the diary of Sir Arthur Throckmorton, who was a contemporary of Sir Walter Raleigh's. The diary was reportedly discovered in a woodshed.

Infamy, too, has its price. Benedict Arnold may be a man whom Americans would like to forget, unless it is a question of letters or papers connected with his treasonous actions. A letter by Samuel Huntington on Arnold's treason was sold at auction for two thousand, one hundred dollars.

Have you ever seen a diary or a signature of Martha Corey's? If you should find one, don't throw it away because you never heard of her. She was one of the "witches" burned at the stake in Salem.

Any name, if it seems at all familiar, is worth checking out. Just because a particular person is unimportant, that does not mean that his signature, even on a letter, is worthless, since the events surrounding that person might have been important.

Documents signed by the judges and important personages connected with the Salem witch trials are of historical importance. Old letters from lawyers discussing specific important cases or points of law can be collectors' items. Even old jury lists have value, especially if they bear handwritten notations.

Letters from any member of the Continental Congress should be checked out, and letters or papers signed by more contemporary Congressmen are also desired.

Presidential signatures are valuable. The collectors desire signatures, letters, papers of all kinds which are handwritten or have affixed signatures of the Presidents. Vice-Presidential signatures, signed letters, etc., also come within the collectors' category. Interesting items, also, are those signed by the wives of the Presidents or their cabinet members or cabinet members' wives.

The signature of a President has always been an important item for a collector. As far back as the 21st day of November, 1864, notice was taken in the *Boston Journal* that one of George Washington's autographs was missing.

Yet an individual does not have to have been President to make his signature famous. Scientists, too, write letters, sign documents and put their names on paper. When Charles Darwin wrote a letter in 1857 that discussed ornithology, it is very doubtful that he would have believed that someday that letter would be worth one hundred and sixty-five dollars.

The Sigmund Freud-Theodore Reik correspondence was sold recently for over thirteen thousand dollars; letters by Albert Einstein sold for even more, because they discussed his unified field theory.

A signature does not have to be that of a famous person to be valuable. Sometimes an autograph can have value simply because the signer was connected with a famous person—Antonio Perez, for instance, of the court of Queen Elizabeth of England. It has been said that he was the man on whom William Shakespeare probably patterned his character Antonio in *The Merchant of Venice*. Today, Perez' signature is very rare.

Shakespeare himself enters the field of autograph hunting, but here, so far, the field has been pretty bare. A writer as prolific as William Shakespeare must have written many letters, scribbled dozens of memos, jotted down hundreds of notes. He must have written thousands and thousands of words, not only the plays, but ideas, notes, etc. There must also have been many business papers signed by him. Therefore, there should be many extant examples of his handwriting. Yet, as far as we can find, William Shakespeare signed his will three times and added two other words. He also signed a few other documents. The sum total of these written records of William Shakespeare is six signatures and two other words. According to one authority, each of these Shakespearean signatures is worth a million dollars apiece.

Other alleged Shakespearean signatures have been listed, by some, as *possible* authentic items. There is also a play with one hundred and fifty lines that was supposedly written by him. If so, it has never been proven. The manuscript of the play, by Sir Thomas More, is still in existence, and is one on which Shakespeare collaborated.

The signatures of writers and artists of all kinds can be included as worthwhile subjects for search. Percy Bysshe Shelley's notebook, for example, brought almost thirty thousand dollars at an auction.

Theatrical personages' autographs are also collectors' items. Movie stars' come into the picture, too, with value depending on rarity and demand. Singers, also! Jenny Lind's signature has been rated as a collectors' item. Circus people and showmen signed papers, too. Phineas T. Barnum would have gotten quite a kick out of the fact that today his signature is a collectors' item.

All kinds of signatures have value. Do you have any old letters relating to the whaling industry, the sea, steamboats, Indians or pioneers? If so, they're worth money to you.

Letters or handwritten or signed documents relating to a famous local or national disaster, such as the Johnstown Flood, are desired items. Letters, signatures and documents relating to heroes, military, pioneer or naval, all have value.

Even letters from soldiers' wives can have value, depending, of course, upon their content, condition, etc. As a matter of fact, any letters from soldiers or officers on either side in the Civil War are collectors' items, their value depending as always on condition, interest and topic of discussion.

It is important in determining the value of military letters whether or not they discuss the events of the war itself, causes, effects or sidelights or whether they discuss home life, relatives and social events. Naturally, the letters discussing the matters connected most directly with the war itself would have the most value.

Letters and documents relating to the Spanish American War have value. As a matter of fact, any document, letter or memo, which relates to any war America has ever been in, has value, depending on historical content, condition and rarity.

Sociological data on matters pertaining to war also have value. For example, sometimes in the South an auction would be held following the death of a plantation owner. If the auction list was signed by the auctioneer or the estate manager and if the auction list has items listing Negroes for sale, complete with the prices asked for them, then that auction list has value. Sometimes such an auction list has value even without a signature on it.

Diaries of famous people, whether historical, literary or political figures, are always desirable. Diaries and journals of early travelers, explorers and wanderers, if their writings are of interest and historical value, are always wanted items.

Where do you look for autographs? Almost anywhere! Books often have autographs on pieces of paper slipped between the pages. Next time you are at an auction or a second-hand bookstore, take another glance at the displays and boxes of used books. It is true that most if not all the books will be worthless—as books. They will not be first editions, nor will they have value as references or textbooks, but if they happen to have a signature inside, as many books do, whether the name of the owner or the name of the giver if the book was a gift, then those books may very well be valuable. The value, of course, would depend on whose name was in the books.

Old valentines are signed, remember! Not only does an old valentine have value of itself, but if the signature on it is that of a famous personage, the signature is worth checking.

Have you ever seen any old money orders with signatures on them? If the signature is that of an important person, then the money order has value to the collectors. Old signed lottery tickets? See if there is a signature on any of them. Then check to see if the signature is that of a famous person, because, if it is, then the ticket has a value to the collector.

Autographs aren't everything, though! Historical documents of all kinds have value and need not necessarily be handwritten. Some are printed. It depends on what they are. Naturally, it helps if a famous person or an individual connected with the historical event described in said document has either signed or initialed it.

Abolition documents or paper items relating to slaves or the slave trade have value. Family papers are desired, provided they give an insight into either a political or a sociological happening of importance for a given time.

Scientists' paper memorabilia are desired. Presidential pardons are not only of value but have given an interesting sidelight into the character of whichever President may have signed them. Even old deeds and printed broadsheets are desired. Old reward posters can be classed as interesting historical documents.

All kinds of historical documents are wanted badly by the collectors but probably the strangest of these items and one which almost anyone can find would be, of all things, old telephone books.

V

THE OVERWEIGHT DIAMOND

Fabulous Lost Gems

AT least half of the largest diamond in the world is missing! Yet the half that we have is so big that, when it was first discovered in South Africa by the surface manager of a mine, Frederick Wells, he thought it was a piece of glass!

Practical jokes had been so prevalent among the mine workers that Wells thought it was just another joke. Rather than make a fool of himself, he had the stone tested first—and then announced his discovery!

Can you blame Wells for doubting that such a stone could be real? It tested out at three thousand, one hundred and six metric carats and weighed approximately a pound and a third. This was the great Cullinan diamond.

It was so big that it could never have been used in its entirety as one stone, but had to be cut into individual gems. Yet even then it was only a part of the original stone. If the entire diamond had been found it would have weighed, according to theory, more than six thousand carats. It would have to have been roughly twice the size of the diamond that was actually found, and, according to one authority, *more* than half of the original stone is missing.

The theory of the missing half of the diamond is based on the form of the diamond. The Cullinan, what was found of it and before it was cut, had three sides that had the natural look of any diamond in the rough, but the last and fourth side was as smooth and clean as though it had been cut.

It is this fourth side that is of particular interest here, since the smoothness of the side as well as the cleanness of the break indicated that somehow, at some time, a piece of the stone had been broken off.

The men in the mine must naturally have looked for the other piece of the diamond when it was realized that they only had part of it, but it was never found. Where is the other piece?

Was it removed from the mine and, considered to be only a piece of glass, a practical joke, was it thrown away? Could it have been used for costume jewelry or sold as a souvenir?

Anything might have happened to the missing piece of the great Cullinan. There is no way of telling, just as there is no way of telling what may have happened to a piece of another diamond found that showed evidences of being only a part of a larger stone. This was the three-hundred-and-twenty-five-carat yellow diamond discovered in Brazil. This stone was flat at one end and fractured as though it had been broken from an even larger stone.

Where is the rest of the stone? How much did it weigh? Has it already been found, or is it still waiting for someone to come along and recover it as a diamond? Or is it possibly already out of Brazil, perhaps having been mistaken for glass and considered to be a useless trinket?

So many famous gems and pieces of jewelry are missing that the amazing thing is that so few are found! For example, in Denmark today there are, preserved on tapestry, the likenesses of two of the early Danish kings, Christian III and Frederick II. Each of the two kings is wearing a crown set with pearls and royal jewels. Yet, today, our only knowledge of these crowns is through the representations of them on the tapestries. Why have they never been found?

All kinds of royal items are missing. Four of the Apostles that were originally on the arches of the Hungarian crown of St. Stephen are missing; in the year 1690, the Great Chain of Office for the City of Dublin disappeared into France. It was taken there by Alderman, later Sir, Thomas McDermott who found it necessary to flee with James II of England. Today, there is not even a description left of the chain. It is thought, however, that the chain was of gold with a pendant representing Charles II.

When James II made his escape attempt from England during the latter part of the seventeenth century, legend states that he took with him the aquamarine that, supposedly, had been set in the *monde* of the English crown. Colonel T. P. Butler, Resident Governor and Major of the Tower of London, feels that there is no evidence to support the story. He affirms, however, the fact that in 1815 the so-called aquamarine then in the crown was found to be nothing but a piece of glass.

Col. Butler feels that a substitution of the glass for the aquamarine could have been made even later than the time of James II. Yet, no matter when it happened, it is a distinct possibility that a change was made—and, if so, then where is the original aquamarine?

All the above gems are, of course, official jewels of record, yet many of the jewels of olden times are known today only through paintings. Hans Holbein, in the early fifteen-hundreds, painted many portraits of famous Englishmen of the day, including Henry VIII. Today our only knowledge of some of the gems that Holbein's subjects are wearing comes from these paintings. Many of these items have completely disappeared.

Many missing gems and items of jewelry have, of course, already been found, and sometimes in the strangest places! The Kohinoor diamond was at one time hidden in the walls of a prison cell and was later discovered there. The Sancy diamond was found hidden in the stomach of a dead man, a royal messenger who had been on his way to the King of France with the gem at the time of his death. He had evidently swallowed the gem rather than let it be taken by robbers.

In a leg wound a slave hid a priceless object, the four-hundred-and-ten-carat Pitt diamond. In desperation, the slave was trying to trade that diamond for his freedom. Instead, he was killed.

The Pitt diamond was eventually cut down to a size of one hundred and forty and a half carats, and was one of the most famous gems in the world, so famous that it was among the French crown jewels that were stolen at the time of the French Revolution.

Not too long after the theft of the crown jewels, however, an unsigned letter was received stating that if anyone was interested in finding the Pitt diamond they might look near the Champs-Elysées.

And that is where they found one of the most famous missing diamonds in the world. In a ditch!

In June of 1651, Dunnottar Castle in Scotland was the resting place of the sword belt for the Scottish Sword of State. However, since this was a time of turmoil, the belt was forgotten. Even its existence was forgotten until 1790, when a descendant of the man who had had it at Dunnottar found it within the garden wall of the ancestral home.

It was also at Dunnottar Castle in 1690 that the Scottish Crown, Sword and Sceptre were saved from the enemy by a woman and her servant, who carried them out right under the enemy's nose. It is said that the lady, a Mrs. Granger, was even helped onto her horse by the enemy commander, and all the while she was carrying the Crown of Scotland concealed under her clothing.

Niccolo de' Niccoli, Renaissance treasure hunter, traveled all over Europe locating old manuscripts and compiling them into a library, which he willed to the public, and which became the beginning of the famous Laurentian Library. Niccoli was also a lover of cameos, and thus when he spotted a cameo suspended from the neck of a poor and very dirty child, he recognized it as an example of great art. The cameo was so fine and so exquisite that it finally became a part of the collection of Lorenzo de' Medici, despite the fact that Niccoli had paid the dirty child very little for it.

Sometimes gems are taken only to be given up a little later. When James II fled to France, he took with him a sapphire that was one inch wide and one and a half inches long. This was the Stuart sapphire, which was eventually given to George III.

It is also possible that an especially important detail of an item may be overlooked. On the blade of the Sword of Scotland there were originally some ornamental leaves; when the leaves broke off, there were revealed gold-filled etchings of two of the Apostles.

Sometimes great historic items are safe, but hidden away for years. In 1707, the regalia of Scotland was locked in a chest in a room in Edinburgh Castle. The room, which had two doors, one of oak and one of iron bars, was locked securely, and the keys were hidden.

One hundred and ten years later, it was decided to open the room and check on the contents of the chest to determine whether or not the regalia was safe. It was even suspected that the crown and jewels were not there, but had been spirited away to England.

It was discovered that the key to the chest was gone. As a matter of fact, the key is still missing, but at that time a warrant was issued and the chest was forced open. Present at this occasion was Sir Walter Scott, who saw for himself that the regalia of Scotland was safe.

Also discovered in the chest was a silver rod, the handle of which was a globe of beautiful rock crystal. It is uncertain, even today, what this rod is. It may have been a Lord Treasurer's mace, or it may have been a Queen's sceptre. No one really knows.

Many gems and jewels are lost forever. Many of the most ancient of the English crown jewels were destroyed during the period following the execution of Charles I, when Cromwell ruled England. Cromwell had the gold and silver of the English regalia melted down, and it was therefore lost to us, although it is true that some of the old gems out of the pre-Cromwellian period were rescued and recovered later, to be placed again as part of the royal regalia of England.

Precious gems have been destroyed by order of the physicians, since at one time it was believed that gem stones had medicinal properties. Lorenzo de' Medici was given crushed rubies, sapphires and other gems in a last desperate effort to save his life.

Gems have also been lost through plain cussedness. There was the diamond weighing forty-seven and a half carats that was ground up, until nothing was left of it but powder, by the express order of the owner, Ali Pasha, the Egyptian viceroy. As Pasha lay dying, he gave the order for the diamond's destruction, willing to see it obliterated rather than let anyone else possess it. This was the fabled Pigot diamond, the Indian gem that once sold for one hundred and fifty thousand dollars in a day when such a price was a veritable fortune.

Occasionally, stories of lost gems and jewelry are nothing more than legends and are therefore to be disregarded. There have been such stories concerning the various portions of the English regalia that was first pawned and then lost during the time of Edward III. It is true that both the jewels and crowns of Edward III and Queen Philippa were pawned. The crowns were pawned to Anthony Bache of France; the Mayor and Commonality of London; William Bishop of London and Richard, Earl of Arundel; and the Corporation of London.

It is true, as we have said, that the crowns and gems were pawned during this time, but none of them were lost in this way. They were all redeemed. In later years some of them were remade or even melted down, but they were not lost in the process of being pawned.

Most stories of lost jewelry, however, have at least a basis of truth. There are also thousands of missing pieces of jewelry about which there is absolutely no story, no record, no remembrance.

There are all kinds of missing antique jewelry items to watch for, with values ranging from pennies to thousands. Watch for beads, bouquet holders, bracelets, boxes for trinkets, charms, combs, cufflinks, earrings, fans, hatpins, match boxes, pomander balls, rings, seals, stickpins, toothpicks of gold or silver and watches. As you can see, jewelry items not only include the items themselves but the accessories as well.

Any item you find is worth checking. If, for instance, you come across old beads that seem to have an Egyptian flavor, don't laugh at their supposedly minute value. They could be one of two things: beads made shortly after the finding of the tomb of Tutankhamen in 1922, many of which were very finely done; or they could be beads dating back to a thousand or so years before Christ, since some ancient Egyptian beads have been restrung and resold in modern markets.

Heirlooms that have been handed down for years can be of inestimable value. Sometimes they have acquired an historic interest far greater than the original owners could have imagined.

Victorian jewelry is still easy to find, especially in the so-called junk boxes in second-hand stores and at rummage sales. Brooches, necklaces and even rings can be found quite often for the price of a quarter.

Even the records of some of the earliest goldsmiths are of importance. Many of these are lost completely. For example, the earliest records of the Worshipful Company of Goldsmiths of London have disappeared without a trace.

As a matter of fact, any item you find might have value—from a giant diamond to a Victorian hair brooch!

VI

TREASURE BEYOND PRICE

The Shroud of Turin

SECONDO Pia stood in the Royal Chapel of the Cathedral of Turin, in Italy. His equipment was ready, his camera was placed and now he waited. The year was 1898.

Spread out to its full length in front of him was a linen burial cloth, about fourteen feet long by about three feet wide. On the Shroud itself, which was the same color as antique ivory, were reddish stains said to be blood. Other marks and stains also covered the Shroud, in shades of browns and whites, showing the frontal and dorsal imprints of a man's body.

Pia was an Italian attorney and photographer. He was more than capable of taking the picture of the Shroud even with the primitive equipment of his day, since he had often taken photographs of old paintings, a subject matter as difficult to do properly as the Shroud.

He was nervous, however. The night before, he had attempted the task of photographing the Shroud, but the opaque glass used to diffuse the arc light had cracked. Now he was ready to try again. He worked carefully. Finally it was over. All he had to do now was to develop the picture.

Pia wasn't nervous any more. The hardest part, that of taking the first known picture of one of the greatest relics in Christendom, was over. When he had the first glass plate in his hand, that is, the first negative, he glanced at it, eager to see how his work had turned out. When he saw what was on the plate, he became so frightened that he almost dropped it.

He knew, of course, that he would see the frontal and dorsal imprints of a man. He knew he would see the blood stains and marks of torture. These had been obvious to the naked eye. What he did not know was that his plate would show that the Shroud was a negative image. Here was the proof that the Shroud was not a painting, as the opponents of its authenticity would have had one believe. It was authentic!

Pia presented the skeptics with a positive photographic image of a man who had died in the agony of crucifixion. There was a frontal and dorsal, full-length image of a man whose feet had been turned inward, with one nail used to nail them to the cross. Nail holes in the hands, which had been folded in death, were clearly visible, as well as the blood that surrounded the areas where the nails had pierced the skin. The traces of blood made by a crown of thorns could be seen, as well as the marks of a wound where the man in the Shroud had been pierced by a lance. There were lashes left by a whip where he had been scourged. Even the man's full beard and mustache showed the blood stains of the terrible agony he had undergone.

All this, of course, Pia could have seen without the aid of the camera—but the camera produced a positive image, proof that the Shroud itself was a negative image actually made by a man's body, and not a painting. Is it any wonder that Pia was frightened? Even though a centuries-old tradition had told him what the Shroud was, no one had told him that the proof of the tradition lay in a modern invention called the camera and that he, Secondo Pia, would be the first to present that proof to the world.

THE Shroud of Turin cannot be traced directly to the first Good Friday, but this is not surprising since no article with a two-thousand-year history could possibly have complete documentation.

The Apostles must have found the Shroud of Christ in the tomb. Probably they hid the Shroud, since that was a time when Christians hid even their faith from their fellow men, unless those men happened to be among the very few Christians then living.

Later, when the Christians were suffering violent persecutions at the hands of Rome, there was even more urgent necessity to hide the

Shroud. Its history is sketchy, yet one authority states that the Shroud was definitely known to be still in existence as early as the 400's.

Eventually it appeared in Constantinople, although no one knows when it first arrived there. It is definitely believed to have been in Constantinople in 1171. Robert de Clary saw the Shroud in Blachernes, which is a suburb of Constantinople, during the time of the Crusades, but earlier the Shroud had been in the private apartments of the Emperor; that is, in 1171.

There was known to be a shroud at Constantinople until the early years of the 1200's, however, and it must have been either similar to or identical with the Shroud of Turin. In 1204 the city of Constantinople was sacked by the Crusaders, and no one really knows what happened to the Shroud after the sacking of the city.

Tradition says that the Crusaders brought the Shroud to Europe in the 1200's. It is a possibility that the Shroud belonged to a gentleman by the name of De la Roche in the early thirteenth century, although this is not certain.

Also, according to one tradition, in 1204 the Shroud was taken on a Crusade. Some records of the Shroud show that it was at Lirey, France, as early as 1300; others, that the Shroud appeared at Lirey in approximately 1354. No one is even certain how the Shroud came to be at Lirey. One thing is certain, however. After the appearance of the Shroud at Lirey, its history is no longer sketchy or uncertain.

In the middle of the fifteenth century, the Shroud was in Chambery, France. Then in 1578 it was taken to Turin, and has been there ever since. The Shroud had been given to the House of Savoy as a gift. The Shroud is still in the possession of the House of Savoy. It is kept at Turin, in the Royal Chapel, which is attached to the Cathedral.

For only one period in recent years has the Shroud been taken from Turin. This was during World War II, when Turin was under threat of bombing. It was decided that the Shroud was not safe there. It was taken to Monte Vergine, also in Italy, and buried deep in a crypt until the danger was over. Today the Shroud is once again in the Royal Chapel at Turin.

There is, of course, no documentary proof that the Shroud at Turin is the same Shroud that disappeared from Constantinople. Yet, whenever it was that mentions of the Shroud entered the records and historical archives of Christianity, it does not really matter. What does matter is the Shroud, which rests today at Turin. What exactly is it?

Is there proof? Is this really the imprint of the body of the Son of God?

Looked at with the naked eye, the Shroud poses a question of faith. The imprint *could* have been painted there. For centuries, no one merely looking at the Shroud could prove that it actually bore the imprint of Christ's body. A man's body, yes, perhaps even Christ's body—but it could have been painted there. Now, thanks to Pia, we can prove that it was not a painting.

Exactly what is the Shroud of Turin? What does it look like? For one thing, it is fourteen feet three inches in length, long enough for a man's body to have been wrapped lengthwise in it. It is three feet seven inches wide.

What about the reddish stains on the Shroud? Are they really blood? Yes, because both visual and photographic observations have been made by doctors, and it has been determined that the spots are actually blood. Some time in the future, it is hoped that spectroscopic examinations can be made. Naturally, with any kind of tests, care must be taken that no damage is done to the cloth.

Theories have been advanced as to the reason why a positive image of the face and body showed up on negative photographic plates. It is thought that the appearance of a *negative* image upon the Shroud itself resulted from a chemical reaction between the cloth, the spices sprinkled over the body, and the urea in Jesus' sweat. Spices were scattered over the body when it was taken down from the cross, and then it was wrapped in the Shroud. The body was not washed or really prepared for burial other than by this sprinkling with spices, because the time of Passover had begun, and Jewish tradition forbade the proper preparation for burial.

Proof that the Shroud really held the imprint of Christ's body was delayed until 1898. It took the camera to prove that the marks on the Shroud had not been painted on. Only tradition and faith surrounded the object until Secondo Pia photographed it, almost two thousand years after it had been wrapped around the body of Christ.

Some cynics would have us believe that the Shroud is a forgery. In answer to those who doubt the authenticity of the Shroud, it should be pointed out that, centuries ago, at the beginning of the Shroud's history, no artist could have known enough, and been enough of a prophet, to have painted a figure on a shroud that would turn out to be a photographic negative. Photography, of course, was not invented until the 1800's.

It is also extremely doubtful whether any artist, either in the past or today in the twentieth century, could have had the technical ability to render the extraordinary image of the face and figure that appeared before the eye of Pia's camera.

Then, too, the details of the story of Christ's crucifixion are completely supported by the markings on the burial cloth. The man in the Shroud had been whipped; his side had been pierced by a lance. He had a beard and a mustache, as Christ had. The man in the Shroud was in his thirties and was six feet tall; an ancient legend states that no man will ever be exactly six feet tall, as was the Christ. The man had the body of an athlete—and it was such a man who used a whip to drive the money-changers out of the Temple.

The man in the Shroud had worn a crown of thorns: not a circlet, but a complete cap of thorns that covered his head. The man had been nailed to the cross, the nails piercing his hands and feet.

At the time of Christ's death, the hands of those doomed to die by crucifixion were either tied or nailed to the wood. The two thieves' hands were tied. Christ's hands were nailed. It was thought that a man whose hands were merely fastened by ropes to the wood died more slowly than one whose hands were nailed. Yet it took Christ three hours to die.

That Christ was nailed to the cross by nails through the palms of his hands was the idea of artists, not scholars. When photographic evidence became available, probably one of the first questions asked by scientists and biblical scholars was, Where were the nail holes? For the scientists knew that only a spot on the wrist would be strong enough to hold the weight of a man's body. And the nails holding the arms of the man in the Shroud had indeed been driven through the wrists.

There was an ancient prophecy that none of the Messiah's bones would be broken. In many cases of crucifixion, the leg bones of the victims were deliberately broken, so that they would not be able to support themselves. When they could no longer brace their feet against the wood, they died quickly. Christ's legs did not have to be broken, because he was already dead. The man who had been wrapped in the Shroud had no broken bones. Thus the ancient prophecy was confirmed.

Another fact may be inferred from the condition of the Shroud. The corpse was obviously unwrapped and taken from the Shroud within a very short time after its burial. Otherwise, the body would have decomposed, and the Shroud would have rotted away.

The Shroud itself, of course, has not come unscathed through the centuries. While it was in Chambery, in the fifteenth century, a fire broke out in the house where it lay. It was being kept in a casket of silver, which, in the intense heat of the fire, began to melt onto the Shroud itself. Attempts were made to put out the fire by throwing water on it, and this, too, left stains. Because the Shroud had been folded, the holes caused by the fire were multiplied at the folds; there are twenty-four holes in all. This very strange-looking damage can still be seen on the Shroud, although the holes have been mended.

There is also—and this is of great interest to treasure hunters— a piece of the Shroud that is missing. This fact explains the absence of part of the imprint of the tops of the feet. At one time, then, the cloth was longer than it is today. The theory is that one of the Byzantine emperors cut off a piece or pieces of the Shroud to give away as gifts.

Some cynic may ask, "How much would the missing piece of the Shroud be worth in dollars and cents, if it could be found?" Such a question does not really deserve an answer, although it is certain to be asked. There can be no monetary value placed upon a piece of the Holy Shroud. Yet, in its way, it could be said to possess more real value than all the gold and gems and lost treasures in the world.

VII

SILVER ON THE C SCALE

Musical Instruments and Lost Scores

EVERY treasure hunter in the world knows the story of the "Strads," the missing Stradivarius violins which mean a fortune to anyone who can find one.

Yet, the finding of a "Strad" is an amusing paradox even to the veteran treasure hunter: since everyone knows about them, there obviously are no "Strads" left—or someone would have found them by now.

The skeptics claim that if anyone, anyone at all, had a "Strad" he would be aware of it because the information is so widely known.

One fact, however, which the skeptics have overlooked completely is that Antonio Stradivari (1644-1737) made approximately eleven hundred violins—yet only about six hundred of them have ever been found!

Simple subtraction shows that there are approximately five hundred Stradivarius violins which have never been found—and five hundred violins simply do not disappear from the face of the earth. Some may have been destroyed, a few may have been damaged beyond repair, but somewhere there are enough "Strads" to make a fortune for anyone who can find them.

The price you could get for a Stradivarius would depend, of course, upon the condition of the instrument. In fine condition it could demand a very high price. I have seen prices for a "Strad" range from $13,000 to $80,000.

45

One other factor that would determine the value of a "Strad" would be the incontrovertible authenticity of the instrument. Naturally, over the years there have been many fakes produced—naturally, because a fake, if it could be palmed off as the genuine article, would bring the maker a great deal of money.

There are, however, various ways by which the experts can tell whether or not a certain instrument is authentic or not.

One method of helping to identify a "Strad" is by comparing the instrument with Stradivari sketches, some of which are in the local museum at Cremona, Italy. Also, the science of acoustics is a great deal of help in identifying authentic "Strads." An acoustical laboratory is being set up in Cremona by the *Scuola Internazionale di Liuteria* for this purpose.

Experts can check the tone of a violin. They can check the "varnish." There are many ways of telling whether or not what you have is actually a "Strad," but before you take your violin to the experts there is one way you yourself can tell whether or not it is at least called a Stradivarius. This is by looking on the *inside* of the instrument.

If you are lucky there will be on the *inside* part of the violin a label, proclaiming it to have been made by Stradivari. Yet here again you must watch for the fake, for it was here that the violin forger marked his model—the label just as much a fake as the violin he had just manufactured.

If you do have a Stradivarius you will have something very rare in the world of music. Before the time of Stradivari (and Nicolò Amati, who taught him) the violin was not the instrument we know today. It had a shrill sound, and it was only the work of these masters that gave their violins the sweet tone which, even today, is considered to be the very finest of violin tones in the world. It has never been excelled.

The shape and size of each piece of a violin are measured to a hair's-breadth in the making, and Stradivari was the master at it. Thus his violins have the magnificent tones that have fascinated music lovers since the 1700's—tones which today can bring you a fortune if you can find a violin that can produce them.

But the "Strad" is not the only violin which the treasure hunter should watch for. It would be rather horrible if, in his search for a "Strad," the treasure hunter should pass by a Guarnerius, because these violins made by Guarnieri are worth many thousands of dollars.

Most authorities rank the Guarnerius violin second to the Stradivarius, although there are many who consider the Guarnerius to be equal to if not better than the "Strad" itself.

Guarnieri was an Italian, born 1683, died 1745. His full name was Giuseppe Antonio Guarnieri del Gesù. The del Gesù part of his name, however, was added as a result of the nickname "del Gesù" which was given to him because he inscribed I.H.S. on his labels— an important fact for the treasure hunter to remember.

There were other members of this family who also made violins, but it is del Gesù whose violins are the most famous and the most valuable and, as a result, the most desired by the treasure hunter.

The Guarnerius violin, the Stradivarius violin, and one other instrument—the Bergonzi cello!

Bergonzi was a pupil of Stradivari and from him learned to make magical instruments that even today are famous both for their extraordinarily beautiful tones and their beautiful shapes.

Every music lover and every owner of a music store wait for the day when they will find a Bergonzi. Such was the case of Jan Paul, owner of a music store in San Francisco, when he purchased six second-hand musical instruments. They had belonged to a musician who was moving and who had to dispose of the instruments.

Paul took all six off his hands for the nominal sum of $2,600. However, when Paul finally had them in his own store, he noticed that one of the cellos seemed different from the rest.

A violin-maker in his own right, Jan Paul examined the instrument carefully. He cleaned it with caution, not really knowing what he might find—but always hoping to find, as every lover of fine instruments does, a rare instrument.

Once the cello was cleaned, Paul realized he had made his find. The instrument was made in 1733 by Carlo Bergonzi of Italy. Over two hundred years old, the instrument was valued at $6,500.

Today there are other Bergonzi cellos missing—each waiting for the treasure hunter to recognize it as one of the most beautiful musical instruments ever made.

WHEN Francis Scott Key first had the inspiration for writing the *Star Spangled Banner* as he watched the attack on Fort McHenry, he had no paper with him and he scribbled the now immortal song on the back of an old letter.

Unfortunately, for the treasure hunter, this letter is now the property of the Walters Art Gallery, and the flag which Key described as "the Star Spangled Banner" is now in the National Museum in Washington, D.C.

However, even if these objects are safely in the hands of the museums, there are "first" copies of the *Star Spangled Banner* which are missing, and which could bring over $3,000 to the treasure hunter if he can find a copy.

The Carr first sheet music edition of the *Banner* should be on your treasure list. These editions have sold for anywhere from $1,000 to over $3,000 each.

At the Parke-Bernet Galleries, New York, a very rare first edition of the *Banner* was recently sold for over $3,000.

Although the actual price paid for this copy is undisclosed, it is known that it was well over $3,000 since there were two other bidders who had quoted above this price, and they had underbid the actual buyer.

Not even the Library of Congress has a first edition of the *Banner,* but maybe you do—in that old trunk in your attic, in the storage bin in the basement, or hidden between the pages of your old family bible.

Prices quoted for the *Banner* are known prices paid for copies which have been held up for auction, but there is much discrepancy in the field of music as to listed prices for rare treasures and the actual prices which the collectors will pay.

In order to sell rare music, you must have an authentic copy first—and then find a collector who wants it badly. Some collectors, for example, would pay almost any price for a collection of Caruso's records on the old Victor label. Others would not give you a dime for them. Jazz lovers are always in the market for the early jazz records, but lovers of classical music would not think they were even worth bidding for.

A point in illustration would be the scores of Victor Herbert, with particular reference to Herbert's operetta, *Prince Ananias.* A copy of *Prince Ananias* could turn up at any time almost anywhere and be sold for as little as $5, yet there is one collector who has gathered together the scores of all of Herbert's operettas—with the exception of the score for *Prince Ananias*. He has made an offer of $100 to anyone who can sell him a copy of it, an offer of two thousand percent over what the score would sell for normally.

It is, therefore, important to find a collector who really wants what you have found. The treasure hunter can only say "It was missing and I have found it. What will you pay for it?"

This, however, would be a simple question for anyone who could find the missing music from *Thespis*, the musical debut of Gilbert and Sullivan, this famous duo of the English operatic stage.

All of the music of *Thespis* has disappeared with the exception of one song, "Little Maid of Arcadee," and one chorus, "Climbing Over Rocky Mountain."

"Little Maid of Arcadee" has not disappeared, because it was published as a separate ballad. "Climbing Over Rocky Mountain" has not disappeared, because it was used again in *The Pirates of Penzance*.

Today, certain collectors badly want the missing parts of the score of *Thespis*. Many people have tried to find this music—and they have failed. Yet perhaps you will be luckier than they and return the missing music from *Thespis* to a world of music lovers who will reach out eagerly for it.

This music of Gilbert and Sullivan would, of course, be valuable, because it is the work of such famous composers, but sometimes missing music is important because it is indicative of a certain period or age from which few examples are extant.

For example, the period of Colonial (pre-Revolutionary) America. During this era many songs were written, yet material from that time is almost negligible in either printed or manuscript form.

Any printed score or musical manuscript from this period would be worth investigation. At least there is one surviving relic of Colonial music. This is a priceless manuscript, dated 1759, which contains four songs by Francis Hopkinson (1737-1791). This manuscript is now in the Library of Congress.

There are, of course, many missing manuscripts, and here, again, as with so much in the music field, the only thing you can say is that they are missing. And if you can find them they will be worth whatever the collectors are willing to pay, and if you are lucky the collectors will be willing to pay a great deal.

A contemporary of Hopkinson's was James Lyon, who was also a composer, and yet, unlike Hopkinson, none of his songs are extant today—unless one might be found in your attic or in that perennial old trunk in the basement.

Another musician from the same period whose works are also missing is William Billings, who wrote secular music.

Another gentleman of roughly the same period (1767-1836) is, however, a musician of some mystery, and we have no idea of whether or not you should look for his music. Not only because there is no way of telling how much the collectors would pay for his missing music, but because we do not know whether or not he ever even wrote music.

Was he a songwriter or wasn't he, is a question which very much bothers the historians of early American music. There is a great deal of doubt as to whether or not this man, by name Johann Christian Gottlieb Graupner, actually composed any music at all. It is a supposition that he did. It is at least known to be a fact that he was one of the leading musicians of the city of Boston, and it seems more than likely that he did compose, but, if he did, his songs have never been found.

Perhaps you will be the one to find a missing song by Graupner—and fill in one of the missing pages of our nation's musical history—and if the collectors want the manuscript badly enough, fill your pocketbook as well.

⫷≼ᏻᏝ≽⫸

VIII

THE FIVE-MILLION-DOLLAR SKULL

Relics of Famous Dead

W HAT would an American pay to get back the Liberty Bell, if it had disappeared? What price would we put on it? Would there be any limit to the amount of money we would give for it?

The answer, of course, is that we would pay to the very limit of our means, since the Liberty Bell has such great significance for Americans. In the same way, the people of Tanganyika would pay any amount for the skull of the Sultan Mkwawa. One version has it that the skull is worth five million dollars to the man who finds it!

The Africans believe that their destiny is intertwined with the destiny of the skull. To own the skull is to rule Africa. They believe that, with the skull, one could control the fate of a continent; without it, they have no sign, no talisman, no "Liberty Bell"!

Where did the skull come from? It has a long and complicated history, dating back to the end of the last century. For many years, the people of Tanganyika had lived in fear of the tribe called the Wahehe. Chief and headman of the Wahehe was Mkwawa, a man whose courage and fighting ability gave him the reputation not only of being unbeatable but of possessing supernatural powers as well. Even when, in 1898, Mkwawa was backed up against a wall and surrounded by his enemies, he refused to capitulate, preferring to die by his own hand. After his death, his skull was preserved.

51

During World War I, the Allies blockaded Germany and thus kept reinforcements from reaching East Africa. The fighting there became hand-to-hand guerrilla combat. The German general, Paul von Lettow, surrendered in 1918.

When the war was over, it was discovered that the skull had disappeared. Rumor had it that the skull had been sent to Berlin. When the British took over German East Africa, the missing skull had taken on vital political significance. It had become so important that a special clause dealing with the matter was put into the Versailles Treaty. The second paragraph of Article 246 of the treaty reads as follows:

> Within the same period (six months) Germany will hand over to His Britannic Majesty's Government the skull of the Sultan Mkwawa, which was removed from the Protectorate of German East Africa and taken to Germany.

Although the treaty demanded that Germany return the skull, she never did return it, but stated that the skull could not be found. There is, of course, another possibility—that Mkwawa's skull was prudently buried in his father's grave, and that the skull the Germans took and never returned was a substitute.

Today, with the new states of Africa rising like the Phoenix, the matter of the skull is again of major importance to the scattered peoples of the new nations. In their struggle for existence, what value would be too high to place on a magic skull that would insure their victory? No one knows for certain how much the people of Africa would pay for the return of the skull, but it is possible that they would pay whatever the seller asked. No one will know until the skull is found and offered for sale!

This gruesome veneration of the skulls or bones of dead heroes and saints runs like a thread through history. The relics of the saints of the Catholic Church are more than collectors' items: they are the physical remains and mementoes of the holiest ones of the Church.

Such relics are so revered by Roman Catholics that when St. Cyprian was being readied for execution, in 258 A.D., the faithful threw pieces of cloth on the ground in front of the block, so that, when he had been beheaded, the blood would flow over the cloths, and they would become relics.

Bones of the saints, strands of their hair, their nail clippings, pieces of their clothing, anything they had handled could be considered relics. In the second century, the bones of St. Ignatius were looked upon as being more valuable than any amount of money.

Even a severed head can be of vast importance! On October 29, 1618, Sir Walter Raleigh joked with the headsman, walked to the place of execution and then gave the order for the ax to fall. When it was over, the head was removed from the block and placed in a red velvet and leather bag. Together with the body, it was removed from the spot in a black mourning coach. The body was buried in St. Margaret's Churchyard, Westminster, but the head was said to have been embalmed and kept by Raleigh's wife until she died. Then his son inherited the head, which was finally buried with him.

The story of Raleigh's head is similar to many that have come down to us over the years—and, like so many stories of this kind, it is impossible to verify. Most of the time stories are kept alive by word of mouth from generation to generation. Sometimes, however, the records of an event are more complete, as is the case with the story of the jawbone of King Richard of England.

In 1766, Gerrard Andrewes, the same Andrewes who was later to become the Dean of Canterbury, was standing near the tomb of Richard II in Westminster Abbey. He noticed a Westminster student pass by very close to the tomb. On watching the student closely, Andrewes discovered to his horror that the young man had pushed his hand into the coffin itself. By the time Andrewes reached him, the young man had the lower jawbone of the king in his hand.

Andrewes rescued the jawbone and kept it; it was preserved in his family, passed from generation to generation, until it was finally returned to the Abbey in 1906. In that year, His Majesty King Edward VII gave his permission to have one of the holes in the side of the tomb reopened. At that time, the Rev. Gerrard Thomas Andrewes replaced the jawbone.

When Richard's tomb was opened earlier, in 1871, a pair of plumbers' shears were found inside; it is thought, because of these shears, which were quite old and marked with the fleur-de-lis, that the tomb had not been opened since the king was buried in 1400. Gone from the tomb, at this opening, was most of the sheet lead that had originally covered the body; the bones, however, were in their correct positions. Twigs placed there four centuries before, as a protection against witchcraft, were found to be undisturbed. All these observations led to the generally accepted belief that the tomb had never been opened. The Westminster student had reached in to take the jawbone through a hole in the side of the tomb rather than through the opening at the top.

Not only do parts of skeletons disappear: sometimes even the graves themselves are lost, and it is not always possible to rediscover them. Walking around a cemetery and reading the names on the old headstones is not always enough. Sometimes a grave has been buried beneath many layers of earth, in a place where even the cemetery has been forgotten.

In California, a wrecking crew was demolishing old buildings to make way for modern improvements. When the shovel dug into the soil at the back of one of the old buildings, the crew found they had turned up a marble tombstone almost a century old, which told a very sad story. It was the headstone of a child, whose entire life had spanned only six months.

If a child's grave and headstone can be forgotten so completely, then even the final resting places of the great men of the past can often be lost for all time—unless a treasure hunter finds them.

For over a hundred years, the remains of one of America's greatest naval heroes lay in a plain coffin in an unmarked grave in France. When John Paul Jones died in 1792, his heroism and patriotism were not as generally recognized as they were in 1905, when experts finally went looking for his grave. They found it in a little cemetery in Paris and removed his remains to the United States Naval Academy at Annapolis, where they are today.

The whereabouts of the grave of Alfred the Great is in some doubt. Legend states that it is somewhere in Winchester, England, but the exact spot is unknown and will remain so until some scholar traces it through research or some treasure hunter finds it.

The sites of the graves of such legendary heroes as King Arthur are often in dispute. Their interest lies in their historic value, but the fascination surrounding the grave increases when its exact location is unknown. Arthur's tomb is supposed to lie in Glastonbury Abbey. Glastonbury Town is the spot where Joseph of Arimathea is said to have planted a cutting from a sacred thorn. Even today, every Christmas Eve, worshipers watch in awe as the famous Glastonbury thorn blooms.

Concerning the first finding of Arthur's tomb in Glastonbury, it is said that a lead cross was discovered, upon which was inscribed the location of the tomb. This led to the finding of the sepulcher itself, which Henry II declared to be the authentic grave of King Arthur.

There are all sorts of legends connected with this alleged first finding of Arthur's tomb. One story relates how the bodies of both Arthur and his wife were originally found in 1191; later, in 1276, they were moved to a final resting place in front of the high altar of the Abbey. Edward I is supposed to have watched the reinterment.

Up until modern times, the actual location of Arthur's tomb was unknown, despite the legend of the first finding. Yet, even while this book was being written, there came reports which astounded the world. C. A. Raleigh Radford, a British archaeologist, announced that he had found the long-lost grave of Arthur.

And, strangely enough, the grave was right where it was supposed to be, at Glastonbury Abbey in England. Once the excavations are completed, and if the hopes for the authenticity of the find are realized, then Arthur's tomb will step out of the realm of fantasy and legend and into the world of historic and verifiable fact.

Even disease and illness have their special meanings for collectors, especially if they were catastrophic diseases like the great plagues. Any item relating to the great London plague would have value today, because the fires that followed the onslaught of the disease not only cleaned out the city—and probably saved the inhabitants from another attack of the plague—but also destroyed many of the mementoes that might otherwise have been saved.

Through the streets of London rolled the carts of the dead, the drivers of these carts calling out their gruesome summonses to the living to bring out their dead. One of these carts would have historical value today.

During the height of the epidemic, red crosses were placed on the doors of the houses where the plague ruled. On each cross were painted prayers begging God for mercy. These crosses are of interest to collectors.

Sometimes, items believed either to cause or to keep away disease or evil are collectible items. As early as the 1400's, hex signs were put up in Europe. Everyone both feared and used the device of the hex sign. These signs served as silent helpers in witchcraft and the black arts. They were believed to protect a man and his family from all the evil influences cast upon him in his everyday life and keep him safe from hunger, disease and the most feared of all illnesses, the plague.

The use of hex signs arose in a day when the people were mostly illiterate. They were often unable to read the few books that did exist. They knew nothing of preventive medicine or hygiene. They only knew that, periodically, sickness and trouble came to them, their only recourse being prayer and the use of the hex sign.

Some authorities argue that hex signs meant little and were intended purely for decoration. However, it does not matter to the treasure hunter which theory is true. The story of the hex signs having been used in conjunction with witchcraft is the more interesting of the two, and it is this theory that is of interest to antique dealers. It lends a certain amount of flavor and mystery to the hex signs themselves, and adds to their value as well—which, is, after all, the important thing to the treasure hunter.

Centuries after these signs appeared in Europe, they began to be found in America. Today we think of them as amusing, interesting and decorative examples of what we call Pennsylvania Dutch folk art.

The Pennsylvania Dutch, actually Germans, settled in Pennsylvania during the very early years of our country's history, and the traditions of their hex signs were brought with them. It is still possible to find American hex signs that are one and two centuries old. To be valuable, they must be in fine condition and rare.

There are still men in the Pennsylvania Dutch area of the country who continue to practice this art, but they become fewer with the years, and it is not their efforts for which the treasure hunter must search. He should watch for the antique American hex signs. These are often still found in the area, painted on barns and farm houses.

Also in this part of the country the treasure hunter may find official paper, such as marriage documents and baptismal certificates; wooden chests and other articles of furniture; even musical instruments, all bearing hex signs, which were intended to ward off the evil eye, illness, or famine and to bring luck to the owner.

It would seem that almost anything connected with disease or the grave has a fascination for the collector and historian.

IX

The Giant and the Lady

The Arms of the Venus de Milo

I
T is said that a dealer once loaded nine hundred camels with the jagged remains of one of the world's greatest treasures, carted the pieces away and sold them as junk.

For centuries these pieces had been lying on the ground, objects of curiosity and wonderment. Where are these pieces today? No one knows. Yet to find one small metal chip of this *objet d'art* would be a treasure hunter's dream come true!

For this was the Colossus of Rhodes, a statue so fantastic in its beauty and so perfectly proportioned that it was considered to be one of the seven wonders of the ancient world. The pieces, if any of them could be found, would be of metal and quite old, since it is thought that the Colossus was finished in about 280 B.C.

The statue was supposed to have been a representation of Apollo. Authorities differ however as to the exact height of the statue, although they agree that it must have been about a hundred feet tall. Some authorities claim that the giant was one hundred and five feet high.

It stood on the Island of Rhodes; it was supposedly so huge that it straddled the harbor. This, however, is probably only a legend; the giant must have stood on one side of the harbor, rather than with a leg on either side.

In 224 B.C., an earthquake hit the Island of Rhodes, shaking the earth so violently that the statue fell to the ground, a masterpiece of the sculptor's art smashed to pieces. And the fragments lay there for centuries, until a junk dealer came and carted them away.

Jagged and broken shards of sculpture may be of little or of great significance, depending upon what piece of sculpture they originally belonged to. Fragments of the Colossus of Rhodes would naturally be of great importance, if they could be found.

There is a man who thinks he can find the missing arms of the Venus de Milo, the famous beauty of the Greek island of Melos. He has already found a piece of a shoulder that probably once belonged to her.

His name is Mathon Kyritsis, Illinois businessman and art connoisseur, who has had personal contact with sources of information not available to most historians and art lovers.

One of these sources was his grandfather, Yiannis Koundourakis, who came to America as an immigrant, bringing with him the legend and some true facts concerning the Venus. One of these tales is that of the peasant Theodore Kendrotas, who discovered the Venus in 1820. He was digging for stones at a spot that was very close to the site of an ancient theatre. This theatre lies beneath the village of Trypiti and near the Klima roadstead.

Stones are usually either rounded off through the action of the elements or have jagged edges due to some accident of nature. When Kendrotas began digging out the larger stones, however, he noticed that these had seemingly been formed by some human process.

They were very ancient and marked by the ravages of time, but even to Kendrotas' untrained eye it was obvious that these stones had one been shaped and intentionally formed by the hand of man. It is possible that Kendrotas did not pay too much attention to the sculpted stones, since there have been so many antiquities found on Melos that a few more unidentifiable pieces of stone might not have meant much to him. He kept digging, however, and eventually discovered the entrance to a cave.

As there are many caves on the island, used by the peasants as storage rooms for household items and for jars of rain water, Kendrotas may have been disappointed at first. But this was no ordinary cave.

When Kendrotas looked inside, he saw art treasures scattered about all over the floor of the cavern—and the most striking of these was the Venus de Milo. A great deal of damage had been done to the statue, yet, according to Mr. Kyritsis, the Venus, when she was first seen in the cave, was standing upright and was intact. At least one other authority states that the Venus was in two parts, but that *the pieces of the arms lay near the statue.*

Whatever version one accepts, it is clear that the Venus de Milo, when found, *did* have her arms. But she did not have them for long!

Both the Turks and the French felt that the statue should belong to their respective governments. When she was placed on a Greek ship bound for Constantinople, the French disputed the Turk's possession of it. In the fight that ensued, the Venus lost her arms. The people of Melos declare that the arms of the Venus fell into the sea and that they are there today, in the harbor of Melos.

Kyritsis, however, by virtue of his particular sources of information, has come to a partially different conclusion. He agrees that parts of the arms must lie under the sea, but he also feels that some portions of them could very well be still on the island.

He bases his theory on observations of a practice that was carried on by many of the islanders. When collectors came to their island to find and purchase antiquities, the people of Melos found that it was possible for them to realize a higher profit from a statue by selling it in parts. The major portion of a statue would be sold to the members of an expedition; later, some "newly discovered" fragments of the same statue would be produced and offered for sale. Kyritsis feels that this is probably what happened to some parts of the Venus' arms, although some pieces were indeed thrown into the sea.

Yet even Kyritsis does not know for sure what position the arms will be in, when and if he finds them. What the Venus was doing with her arms is a question that has been argued ever since the statue was first brought to public notice in the early 1800's.

Some say she was carrying a spear or an apple; perhaps she was spinning; perhaps she was touching the folds of her clothing. Mathon Kyritsis' theory is that the Venus was holding an apple in one hand and touching her clothing with the other. This description was given to him when he was in his teens by John Tatarakis, who was then a very old man. Tatarakis stated that the Venus was holding the apple as though she were in the act of eating it. This, of course, would explain the extreme upward slope of her left shoulder.

The details of Tatarakis' description of the Venus were particularly intriguing. The apple she held was the Apple of Discord fabled in mythology. Upon the apple, he said, was the inscription, *"Ti Kalisti Laveto,"* or, "Let this belong to the most beautiful."

With the stories of Tatarakis and of his grandfather ringing in his ears, there was only one thing for Kyritsis to do. And so, in 1961, he set out to find the arms of the Venus de Milo.

Jim Thorne and Robert Kendall, both expert frogmen, went with him to Melos, where they made preliminary underwater investigations. The search was not successful, however, at least as far as the arms were concerned. They did find the remains of some ancient buildings under the sea, about three hundred feet from shore, and other ruins even farther out. But this did not assuage Kyritsis' feelings of disappointment.

After this unsuccessful attempt, he turned to another source of information on Melos: he asked the people of the island to help him. It did not matter, he told them, if what they turned up did not seem important—it might still prove to be valuable as a lead, a clue to the whereabouts of the fabled arms.

The islanders began to search their homes, their barns, the caves where they stored their water. One of the women had an old vase that she had been using for household purposes. Since it was obviously very old, she thought Kyritsis might want to see it. He was able to identify it as the very vase that had been standing in front of the Venus when she was first seen by Kendrotas. A piece of a carved marble shoulder was also found which will have to be carefully checked to verify whether it once actually belonged to the Venus.

Heartened by these finds, Kyritsis decided to try again for the arms. Even as this book is being written, he is on his way to the island of Melos, to try his luck both on land and under the sea, this time in the company of several Greek sponge divers, chosen for their familiarity with the underwater terrain.

Before Kyritsis left for Melos, he received word from his brother that he had already located something of importance there. The disclosure awaited the arrival of Kyritsis in person.

By the time this book is printed, the arms of the Venus may well have been found!

X

THE MASTER'S TOUCH

Paintings by the Masters

THE room is hushed and quiet. There is only the heavy breathing of the men who are bending over an object which takes all their attention. The smell of chemicals fills the air—turpentine and alcohol; sulphuric acid; cedar oil and oil of spice. Small instruments lie ready to puncture tiny spots on the object, which is still untouched by the silent, eager men.

Suddenly the door opens and attendants wheel in an X-ray machine. The men are ready to begin. Their work is quiet; yet there is an urgency in the air, an urgency caused by the knowledge that the slightest miscalculation on their part may do irreparable damage. Their movements are calculatingly slow—because any spilling of their chemicals or slip of their instruments may cause untold damage.

The X-ray apparatus is brought forward and focused on the object they have been studying so carefully. Finally, then, they know what they have before them—and what they must do. They know that for months they will be in this room working with chemicals and instruments, and, using all their talents, they will scrape and clean and bring to life the object which they have so anxiously studied.

For what they have before them is a painting, but not just any painting. It is a very bad, poorly painted portrait. Yet by the use of chemicals and X rays they know that underneath this badly done work is another painting, a fantastic find in the world of art. A painting by one of the old masters, its marvellous colors and fabulous brush work hidden by the workings of an inferior artist who had placed his own splotchy work on top of one of the world's masterpieces because he had been too poor to buy canvas.

This is what has probably happened to many of the masterpieces of yesteryear. Where are they now? Perhaps in your attic is an old painting worthless in itself, yet beneath the top layer of paint is another painting, a painting so valuable that it could pay for your next yacht or two—if you only knew it.

So take a good, a really good, look at that old painting of yours. Perhaps you really have something.

Sometimes you can tell at a glance that one painting is underneath another one, because the top layer of paint has been damaged in some way and the older painting shows through. Most of the time, however, it takes an expert to tell, and it takes an expert to clean away the top layer of paint. Never, never try to remove it yourself. This could cause irreparable damage to the bottom painting, and irreparable damage to the value of the finer of the two paintings, a point of great importance to the treasure hunter.

There are some people who will insist upon trying a do-it-yourself method, by applying the more common paint removers such as alcohol, soap with potash, alkali or acetic acid, but remember that all of these regular paint removers remove paint at such a speed that the painting itself can become damaged. Only the experts can use the proper chemicals at the proper speed.

Only the experts can really do anything with these double paintings. They know when and how to use the proper instruments, chemicals and X-ray machine. They know all the modern ways of determining the authenticity as well as the number of layers of paint on a canvas.

X rays pass through the atom structure of the painting, and the less atoms present the easier it is for X rays to pass directly through. If there is one painting directly over another, it is harder for the X rays to penetrate both than if there were only one painting present. Thus the X ray finds the existence of the second, underneath painting.

Also, by seeing which parts of the painting the rays can penetrate most easily, the experts are able to tell quite easily whether a whole painting has been painted over or only a part of the original painting has been retouched. The latter is frequently found to be the case, since it was often simpler merely to change an older painting and bring it up to date than to paint an entirely new one.

The more prevalent custom, however, was for the artist to paint over the entire painting, leaving his own, usually hopeless, endeavor on top of what would be an enduring work of art to be hung proudly in museum halls—if it could be found.

How many paintings were lost in this way no one really knows. But there is at least one painting which may fall into this category. This is the portrait of Cesare Borgia by Pier di Lorenzo.

This painting has completely disappeared; yet, if it could be found, it would be a museum piece. Over four hundred and fifty years old, the painting may very well have been painted over. It certainly disappeared during a period when artists were notoriously poor and hungry, and any canvas within reach became the background for their art.

The portrait of the Borgia had already disappeared in the sixteenth century, in the days when canvas was still rare and expensive, so the probability is that somewhere the painting is well hidden beneath a layer of more modern art.

The portrait, of course, might not have been painted over at all but might still be in its original state. It could be that the eyes of a Borgia still stare out at a make-believe Renaissance world from the dark corner of someone's attic.

If your attic does contain this painting, it contains not just a painting by a master but the portrait of a man who made history; a man of the Renaissance who, among other things, has been accused of killing his own brother, although historians disagree on this point.

Soldier and Cardinal of the Roman Catholic Church, this then is the man that Pier di Lorenzo painted. Perhaps, if you are lucky enough, this painting is in your attic, in your basement, or in the neighborhood second-hand store, either unrecognized in its original state or painted over by a mediocre artist too poor to buy a new canvas. If so, it is just waiting for you to take it to the experts, who, with their chemicals, their instruments, and their X-ray machines, can clean and repair it.

Such was the case in the little church of Lucignano d'Arbia near Siena when the priest decided that the rather mediocre and very dirty painting above the altar needed repairing.

It was a very old, mediocre painting, but the desire for neatness if not religious compunction decided the priest to have it restored. When the workmen began on the painting, however, flakes of paint came off to reveal an eye beneath the outer layer of paint. With dispatch the painting was forwarded to Rome's Restoration Institute, where it was properly restored and cleaned over a period of many months.

When they were finished, they had uncovered the lost Madonna and Child by Simone Martini, Italian painter of the later 1200's and early 1300's. This was one of the greatest finds in art history.

Perhaps then, if you are lucky enough, that old painting you have may be the Borgia by di Lorenzo, and it will become another milestone in the history of paintings once lost, but now found and replaced by the treasure hunters of the world.

I N the world of painting is one name which is familiar to many: Cuyp, the very famous family of Dutch painters who lived and worked in the 1500's and 1600's. Their works are listed among the great masterpieces of all time.

Yet, as with many of the great masters, there was at least one of their paintings which had disappeared—a painting of the embarkation of the Pilgrims for America. It is thought that this painting was an artistic representation of the actual scene itself, so that for all time the faces of the Pilgrim Fathers would be captured for posterity.

For many years this painting had been lost, until one day it was relocated by another painter who, strangely enough, was George H. Boughton, the man who himself painted such scenes as "The Puritans Going To Church" and "The Return Of The Mayflower."

How odd a coincidence that Boughton, who himself painted the Pilgrims, should have been the man to locate what was probably the only accurate representation of what the Pilgrims really looked like. Or perhaps it was the other way round, and Boughton found the Cuyp painting first and it inspired him to paint the Pilgrims.

Whatever happened, he had found one of the lost art treasures of the world. Its value? It would be impossible to judge the value of this particular painting today, but recently a Cuyp painting sold for $71,400.

Yet this was only one of the lost paintings, for there must be many hundreds of them if it were possible to list and catalogue them. The simplest way, of course, to search for lost paintings is to watch for the signature of the artist on any painting which you might find.

To list all of these artists would be impossible without writing a complete book on this subject; but below are a few names of different periods and nationalities, together with some definite lost paintings. Also included are prices of paintings which are not lost but which give some indication of the value of a particular artist's work.

Peter Paul Rubens. A painter whose works bring fabulous prices. Recently one of his paintings sold for $770,000.

Paul Cézanne. One of his paintings recently sold for over $400,000, another for $616,000, and yet another for $252,000.

Vincent van Gogh. One of his paintings sold for almost $400,000.

Edouard Manet. One of his paintings sold for $316,400.

El Greco. One of his paintings sold recently for over $200,000.

Pablo Picasso. One of his paintings sold for $152,000.

Modigliani. One of his paintings recently sold for over $57,000.

George Inness. A painter whose works are always in demand, works which, when discovered, find their places readily in galleries and museums. Already there are five of his paintings in the Metropolitan Museum in New York City.

Edgar Degas. His painting "After The Bath" was stolen from the Milwaukee Art Institute. While it is difficult to appraise this painting, I have seen the value quoted at $6,000.

John Singleton Copley. Recently an estimate of over $2,500 was placed on one of his paintings.

Katsushika Hokusai. A Japanese artist who produced so many paintings that anyone could have one of them without even knowing it, especially since they were so little thought of in his own country that they were used as wrapping paper for exports. If you should find a Hokusai, however, remember that it would have to be in good condition and neither torn nor wrinkled, for it to have any great value.

Evert Duyckinck (the First). An early American painter, ALL of whose works are known to be missing. In this case, however, there is no way of knowing how much value his paintings would have until one has been found and has been appraised by the experts.

Rembrandt van Rijn. Last but by no means least, this great Dutch master's painting "Aristotle Contemplating the Bust of Homer" was recently sold at auction to New York's Metropolitan Museum for $2,300,000!

There is of course no way of telling, for example, that Degas or Rubens or El Greco painted such and such a number of paintings and that such and such a number are now missing. This would be an impossibility, but there is a very good chance that these artists did paint works, especially during their younger and struggling days, that have never been found.

Watch for their signatures on any painting that you find, and, even if you personally do not care for it, remember that the average person is not an art connoisseur. The question of the beauty and fame of a painting rests with the art critics, the museum curators, and the collectors.

Watch especially for the paintings of the Impressionists, works by such masters as Cézanne, Pissarro, Sisler and Renoir. Many years passed before these men were recognized. Their works were laughed at and ridiculed. No one wanted them. No one liked them. No one would buy them. There is no way of telling how many of their paintings were lost because of the little value they had at that time.

Watch for paintings by all of the great masters of the past. That old painting which you thought so little of might turn out to be one of the finest examples of the master's touch the world has ever seen. Tomorrow it might be hanging in the gallery of a famous museum —and you will be out buying your first yacht.

XI

TREASURE IN THE TRUNK

Advertisements and Artifacts of Yesteryear

THAT old trunk up in your attic could conceivably contain almost anything, even a scrap of paper mentioning Old Crow whiskey—and, if so, that scrap of paper might be worth two hundred and fifty dollars to you.

The Old Crow Historical Bureau of the Old Crow Distillery Company is offering a standing reward of two hundred and fifty dollars for authentic documents, especially ones that relate famous nineteenth-century Americans to Old Crow whiskey.

All kinds of items have been found and turned in to the company. A notice of a ship that was carrying Old Crow having arrived safely in port was located. An advertisement for an inn promised travelers not only warm beds and good food, but that they would be served James Crow's bourbon. One printed item offered a reward of five dollars and a drink of Old Crow for the return of a red cow who had lost her tail.

What the bureau is mainly interested in, however, are items that show that famous persons of the last century drank and appreciated Old Crow whiskey. In a newspaper was found an account of Jack London toasting a friend with Old Crow. Another newspaper article stated that "Andy Jackson" praised Old Crow. A letter was found, stating that the famous writer O. Henry referred to Old Crow whiskey as "superb." Daniel Webster was proven to have been a fancier of Old Crow, as it was shown that roast beef and Old Crow were served following one of his debates.

Old Crow quotes could be found in many places—in diaries, newspaper testimonials, or printed advertisements. Remember that Old Crow whiskey was sometimes referred to as James Crow's whiskey or James Crow's bourbon. Any document found must, of course, be accepted by the bureau in order to entitle the finder to the reward.

Anyone who has Old Crow items should write to the Old Crow Historical Bureau, 380 Madison Avenue, New York City; or 99 Park Avenue, New York City. The bureau, of course, specializes in Old Crow items. There are other collectors who desire any kind of old whiskey or saloon item.

The bars themselves, with their mellow mirrors and smooth wood surfaces, are valuable items today. Fine bars in good condition can bring hundreds of dollars at auctions.

Old-fashioned saloon signs were often made of tin, but the rarest—and therefore the most valuable to the collector—were of porcelain. These porcelain signs were curved, so that they could be seen from all sides, and they were hung either outside, on a corner of the building, or inside the barroom itself.

Almost anything that is even remotely connected with the liquor trade can have value to collectors. A sixteen-inch-high, polychrome wine keg with a figure sitting astride of it recently sold for one thousand, five hundred dollars at an auction. This item was not even a real wine keg, but merely a small statue of a keg with human rider.

Old advertisements can be valuable—Underwood Deviled Ham ads, for example, most of which date from before 1900. Do you remember the old tin trays with advertising on them that were so popular at one time? They are collectors' items today. These trays were manufactured mainly in Ohio in the early 1900's. The desirability of such a tray would depend on what product it advertised.

Magazine ads can also have some value, such as the old Lion and Arbuckle Coffee ads. Also watch for Lion and Arbuckle advertising cards and paper cartons. These old cartons sell today for as much as two dollars apiece. In the old days, the lion on the face of the Lion and Arbuckle carton could be removed and saved, as today we save trading stamps. The Arbuckle lions were traded for bicycles or French harps. Today they can be traded for cash to the collectors.

Whatever the business or profession of yesteryear, it left mementoes—and these have become collectors' items. Old vending machines are highly prized. These must be automatic and must have been made before 1920. Have you any old printers' catalogues? They may have some value. Even sundials are desired, considered to be of interest to clock enthusiasts or scientific instrument collectors.

To most people, Wall Street means the center of American trade and business—but, to the collector, it means a whole list of collectible items. Cartoons, prints, books, anything that depicts the past history of the Street is fair game for the collector of Wall Street items.

Certain old typewriters are now considered to be collectors' items. There were typewriters in existence before the 1900's, examples of which may be found in American museums. In the year 1714, in Great Britain, a patent for a typing machine was requested by one Henry Mill. No Mill machine is in existence today—unless you can find one. Even the drawings for his typing machine have disappeared.

Have you any strange old mouse traps around the house? There is a gentleman who collects them, if you do. This collector has been unsuccessful in locating certain types of old mouse traps. Perhaps the one in your attic is just the one he is looking for.

Telescopes and other instruments that were used in astronomical studies are desired. Museums and historical bureaus want antique items in the scientific fields, including those once used by dentists, druggists, and doctors.

The druggists' show globes that were once so common are now beginning to find their way into the hands of collectors. Mortars and pestles, those symbols of the pharmacist's trade, are some of the most interesting and beautiful items collectors prize. Some of these mortars and pestles are fine enough to be museum pieces. They were made of glass, stone, wood, and various metals, including pewter.

When the older drugstores in small towns sell out their stock, this provides one with a good opportunity to find items of this kind, as well as old medicine bottles and even old patent medicines, which are collectible. Medical instruments, such as bleeders, and accessories, such as measures and spoons, come under the heading of collectors' items. Old medical charts are desired, as are old magazines and books on health and other subjects. And did you ever see any of the old advertisements showing the medicines of the early and middle 1800's? These, too, are of value.

Medicinal rings, also collectors' items, were rings that had been blessed by a saint and therefore had great power to cure diseases. They were in use for hundreds and hundreds of years, and today some of these rings are museum pieces. Several centuries ago, it was a custom for the kings and queens of England to give away rings on Good Friday. These rings had been blessed, and were called cramp rings. They were worn as cures for epilepsy.

Do you happen to have an antique velvet-lined case filled with ivory- or mother-of-pearl-handled dental instruments? If so, then you have a collectors' item.

As a matter of fact, anything pertaining to early dentistry has some value today—medals, figurines, illness dishes, dentifrice containers, etc. Do you have any old books on teeth? These are on the wanted list, especially those printed before 1850. Photographs and prints having to do with dentistry are desired. The patron saint of dentistry is St. Apollonia, and today items pertaining to this saint are collectible.

False teeth, or dentures in polite parlance, are not a modern invention. In the middle 1700's, an ingenious dentist carved the base and back teeth for a denture out of a hippopotamus tusk, then attached human teeth to the front of the base. The same dentist made denture bases entirely of gold. Teeth were attached to the base, and the front of the base was then painted with flesh-colored paint, so that the gold would not shine when the wearer was speaking or laughing. Dentures have also been made of ivory.

Occasionally old dental chairs with crank handles are sent to the junkyard when old offices are dismantled. They are collectors' items, however, and should not be destroyed in this way. They're worth money to you, if you can find and salvage them.

There are rare and valuable figures of dentists at work on their patients that may be found today. Some of these are very old and are made of fine French or German porcelain.

Even old toothbrushes are on the collectors' list. From letters about whiskey to old toothbrushes—if you can find them, they are worth cold, hard cash.

XII

THE GREATEST TREASURE OF THEM ALL

The Story of the Holy Grail

IT is the year 1910, near the world-famous city of Antioch in Syria. Workmen labor at the digging of a well, and, as the work proceeds, the piles of dirt taken out of the ground grow higher and higher.

Suddenly the work stops, as one of the workmen spots a gleam of metal shining in the sunlight. Carefully he and his companions remove it from the surrounding dirt.

As they scrape away the centuries-old crusty residue, they find that they have unearthed two cups, one set within the other. The inner cup is very plain and unprepossessing, but the outer cup is made of silver.

The cups pass out of their hands and into the possession of the experts. Slowly the word spreads, and museum curators and historians from all over turn their eyes toward the two cups, for now the word is out that perhaps here, near the city of Antioch, in the year of Our Lord one thousand nine hundred and ten, the greatest treasure of them all has been found. For it is believed that the inner cup might be that most fabulous of all treasures—the Holy Grail!

The experts argued and examined and tested, and for a long time the only thing upon which they agreed at all was to disagree. Certainly the legends of the Holy Grail bore out the possibility of the finding of the cup somewhere near Antioch, for almost immediately after the Last Supper the cup had passed out of the hands of Christ and into the possession of Joseph of Arimathea.

It is said that Joseph caught in this cup the blood that flowed from Christ's wounds as he was dying. The legend goes on to tell of the miraculous transportation of Joseph to England—and with him went the Grail, which ever after was miraculously filled with food and drink for Joseph.

Then for many centuries the stories of the Grail are concerned mainly with men's attempt to find it. The Knights of the Round Table made the search for the Grail a part of their chivalric code. Everyone knows the story of Galahad, the pure in heart, who saw the Grail.

Certainly, aside from these legends, there seems to be a good foundation for the idea that the Grail was taken to England by Joseph of Arimathea. The legend of the Grail was known in West Britain even before the days when the inhabitants were converted to Christianity.

But after Galahad? What happened to it then? According to the legend, the Crusaders actually had the Grail. With it in their possession they marched toward the Holy Land, and one of their purposes was to once more replace the Grail in the land from whence it originally came.

Yet their hopes were greater than their fortunes, because they were both outnumbered and outfought. But even in defeat their thought was of the Grail. Rather than let it fall into the hands of the enemy they buried it—near Antioch.

And it was here that the workmen dug their well and unearthed the cup that for a while excited every museum curator in the world. It was a lovely cup, too, even though when cleaned it was found to be damaged by corrosion. It was cleaned by the finest experts in the field, and today it is a lovely object. The inner cup is very plain, but the outer cup is of chased silver portraying vines and figures and grapes, all of them woven into an artistic setting which is still lovely even after all the centuries it lay in dust and dirt.

Today, this cup is in the possession of the Metropolitan Museum in New York City and it can be seen there at any time. It is called the "Antioch Chalice," because, unfortunately for the world but fortunately for the treasure hunter, it has been finally decided that this cup is *not* the Holy Grail.

It took exhaustive tests, a great deal of research, and the varied opinions of many many experts before this decision was finally reached, but today the authorities of the Metropolitan Museum of Art reject the theory that it is the Grail.

They list the age of the Antioch Chalice as being of the fourth or possibly fifth century, very early Christian work certainly, but they deny that the inner cup is the one out of which Jesus actually drank.

If this then is not the Holy Grail, then the Grail is still among the missing treasures of the world. One cannot imagine the price which men could ask for this holiest of all the drinking cups of the ages!

Yet, certainly, the finding of the Grail would have much more far-reaching effects than the monetary reward it might bring, for this is the cup to which the knights of the Middle Ages dedicated their whole lives, the cup for which the crusaders gave their lives.

This is the cup which, if found, would bring into actuality the legends which have followed its existence for almost two thousand years.

For this is the cup out of which Christ drank at the Last Supper. It stood on the same table where Christ broke bread with his Apostles. This is the cup that has been searched for by more people than any other lost treasure in the world.

There is no museum curator, no expert, no historian who could turn his back on it—if you could find it.

For now, after the original excitement of the finding of the Antioch Chalice, after the disappointment when it was finally determined that it was not the Holy Grail, the experts are more aware than ever that someday the Grail may still be found.

And until the day comes, the Holy Grail must remain the most important lost treasure in the world.

XIII

Treasure in the Junkyard

Carriages, Coaches, and Cars

PEDESTRIANS watched breathlessly as the strange-looking vehicle came hurtling down the road like a juggernaut of fantastic speed. Missing the now screaming onlookers by inches, the vehicle hurtled toward a brick wall. Nothing could stop the inevitable. Unable to come to a halt, the vehicle plunged into the brick wall—and the wall tumbled down.

Police arrived on the scene and, as usual in these cases, argument and discussion ensued with voices raised loud and anger rampant. The man had been speeding—of this the police were certain. But they were not as sure of themselves and of their laws against speeding as policemen of today would be—for this was the year 1769.

The vehicle, which was probably the first one ever involved in the misdemeanor of speeding, is lost. It would be, if you could find it today, one of the greatest finds in the history of antique-car treasure hunting.

Made by Captain Cugnot in 1769, it would be an historic find in this field, similar in value, possibly, to the steam artillery-carriage made a year later in 1770 by this same Captain Cugnot, a man undaunted by his previous set-to with the law.

Today the steam artillery-carriage is in the *Conservatoire National des Arts et Métiers* in Paris, France, an historic relic of the world's automotive past. But Cugnot's other car? It is one of the most fabulous missing automobile treasures.

Many early vehicles like Cugnot's steam artillery-carriage, however, are in museums and collections. In the United States National
Museum is the first successful gasoline car built in America. Conceived by one brother and built by another, this vehicle is an American first. It was Charles E. Duryea who conceived the idea for the
car, and his brother, J. Frank Duryea, who built it.

In the *Deutsches Museum* in Munich, Germany, there is a vehicle which owed its existence to two men. It is a three-wheeler built
in 1885 by Carl Benz with an engine by Gottlieb Daimler, the man
who developed the high-speed gasoline power plant which Benz
used in the three-wheeler.

One inventor in this category of extant cars had great hopes for
his machine. He called it *L'Obeissante* which means, of course, the
Obedient. This was the steam coach built in 1873 by Amédée Bol-
lec. This coach is now in the *Conservatoire National*, Paris.

In the Henry Ford Museum in Dearborn, Michigan, is a steam
buggy made during the Civil War period by Sylvester H. Roper.

There are many, many of these rare examples in museums today,
but there are others, like the 1769 Cugnot vehicle, which have never
been found. Coaches belonging to such men as Sir Charles Dance,
Maceroni, Summers, J. Scott Russell, and Church, have disappeared. Other men, too, made vehicles which today have gone the
way of so many things of the past. The coaches, for example, of both
Squire and Ogle have completely disappeared. Not one of these
vehicles is known to exist, and they are among the lost treasures of
the antique-car field. Find just one of them, and you are on the road
to fortune.

Also missing are the coaches of Goldsworthy Gurney; the coaches
of Walter Hancock, the man who first made use of the hand brake;
and the coaches of W. H. James, famous for his introduction of the
variable-ratio transmission. Any of the coaches made by these men
would be worth money in your pocket if you could find them.

These missing coaches were English, built between 1820 and
1840. They were steam stagecoaches, on their way to becoming
numerous when opposition was raised to them mainly by owners
of railroads and conventional stagecoach lines. They simply could
not stand the competition from the better steam stagecoaches.

A law was passed—the so-called red-flag law—which insisted, not
only that the steam stagecoaches be preceded by a man walking

with a red flag in his hand, but that the speed of the coaches be limited to four miles an hour.

So the steam stagecoaches passed from England's roads, but today, if you spot one, hang on to it, for these vehicles are among the most sought-after collectors' items in this field.

But do not stop there. Watch for any old car. The one you thought was junk might turn out to be priceless. It is of course hard to place a definite market value on any specific car. The value would depend on age, rarity, condition, and how badly the collectors want it.

Antique-car collecting has become a craze in America in recent years. Our automotive civilization likes to remember its past. There are already some fabulous collections—like the Long Island Automobile Museum, the exhibit at the Museum of Science and Industry in Chicago, the exhibit at the Smithsonian Institution, and the famous Harrah's Collection. The collections grow, and the craze continues.

So take another look at that old car which you saw the other day in your neighborhood junkyard. Maybe it was not just another old car—maybe it was really a collector's item worth a fortune!

HOW much is that old car you saw in the junkyard really worth? It might be worth $5. It might be worth $50. It might be worth $5,000—depending, again, on condition, rarity, make and age.

At least one old car was evaluated at $10,000 by the insurance appraisers. Unhappily for the insurance company who set this evaluation, the car was burnt in a fire that destroyed it while it was on display as an exhibit in the 1929 Los Angeles Auto Show.

This was a 1901 Packard, one of five models which were made that year, models which were all two-passenger cars and had one-cylinder engines and wheel bases of seventy-five inches.

That there were five of these models made we know from the records of the Studebaker-Packard Corporation in South Bend, Indiana. What we do not know is where all of these cars are today. One of them, of course, was the one destroyed in the Auto Show. We also know that several years ago Mr. Henry Joy of Detroit, Michigan, purchased a second 1901 Packard. This leaves three 1901 Packards not accounted for.

They could, of course, already be in the hands of the collectors.

It would be impossible, however, to ascertain this without writing to every museum, every collector, and every old-car enthusiast in the world. Obviously, this would be impossible.

The logical thing would be to simply remember the 1901 Packard and watch for it. That old car which you thought was junk might turn out to be a $10,000 horseless carriage that collectors would give their eye teeth to have.

Any car from the early 1900's is worth checking, and, strangely enough, these cars are not as scarce as most people think. In 1901, the same year as the 1901 Packard, there were 14,800 passenger cars registered in the United States, and each one is a potential missing treasure varying in value from $10 to $10,000, depending of course on rarity and condition.

Not only cars from the early 1900's can be of value—any make of early car can be worth something. There have been so many kinds of cars made in America, over 2,600 kinds, that chances of finding a collector's item are good.

Sometimes these early cars are destroyed and a treasure is lost forever. Sometimes the loss of the car is accidental, as with the 1901 Packard destroyed in the Auto Show.

Sometimes, however, the loss of the car is just plain thoughtlessness—like the car which was used, in the first American automobile race, by Frank Duryea. Duryea made racing history when he won the race, but years later treasure history was also made when the car was junked—a loss to treasure hunters and collectors that can never be replaced.

Sometimes a car may even be destroyed for patriotic reasons. When World War II broke out, the grandson of Alexander Winton, one of our first automobile builders, gave his grandfather's first automobile to the scrap drive—and it was lost forever.

The treasure hunter must never destroy a car or junk it until he knows what it is. What you think is junk might be considered a treasure by the collectors.

Things are being destroyed today which may be of value some day in the future—if they could be preserved. Antique fire engines have been scrapped in countless numbers, because fire departments either sold them or used them for parts long before they reached the antique-car category. Their value would probably be small today, although there are many good specimens already in museums. What they would be worth in the future if they could be preserved, no one knows, but probably a great deal—if you find one and preserve it.

The transportation of the pioneers has also suffered from this thoughtlessness. Conestoga wagons wore out or were left to rot. And on the rivers the early steamboats of the waterway pioneers were left to rot, sold for lumber, or destroyed by unthinking Tom Sawyerish juveniles.

These objects are rapidly disappearing from the scene, to be forgotten forever unless the treasure hunter does something about it. For, if he can stop the destruction, he is on his way to placing examples of an almost forgotten way of life in the hands of the collectors—and money in his pocket.

XIV

THEY WENT THAT-A-WAY

Mementoes of the Old West

DO you own anything that belonged to "The Fighting Pimps"?
Or do you have something that was used or owned by Big
Nose Kate? If so, what you have is an honest-to-goodness piece of
Americana.

"The Fighting Pimps" was the nickname given to Wyatt Earp and
Bat Masterson, because of the fact that they spent so much of their
time in houses of ill fame, in the company of such ladies as Big Nose
Kate Fisher, whose major claim to fame is that she was the common-
law wife of another famous westerner, Doc Holliday.

It has not been as long as it seems since the days of the gun-fighters.
Wyatt Earp was still alive in the 1920's. And anything that belonged
to him or to his associates has value. The men and women of this
heroic time in our nation's past were persons of stature. They opened
a new and brutal land; they bled and died on the streets of the
frontier towns; they opened vast new territories to civilization. Remember their names, for they were some of the men about whom the
legends of the Old West were written.

> Billy the Kid
> Bob Ford
> Wild Bill Hickock
> Frank James

Jesse James
William Quantrill
Johnny Ringo
Cole Younger
Jim Younger

Another name may not be familiar to readers of today, that of Jane Burke, a mail carrier between Deadwood, South Dakota, and Custer, Montana. She has become famous as Calamity Jane, Indian scout and aide to General Custer. Anything that she owned or wore would now be a collectors' item.

The cook, the gambler, the cowboy, they all left their mementoes. Old chuckwagons, the forerunners of today's trailer kitchens, had built-in cupboards and spaces to hold potatoes, fruit, and cooking utensils. Today these belong in the museum. Also watch for western saddles, which were of various types, depending on what part of the country they were used in.

Hitching posts, horse collars and branding irons are all collectors' items. Harry "Hap" Magee of Danville, California, is one of America's foremost collectors of branding irons, having accumulated over six hundred of these. According to Mr. Magee, the branding irons used in the old missions have the greatest value to the collector. One of his most prized possessions is a mission iron used in the 1700's.

Branding irons are native to many countries, including Mexico, Spain, Canada, and Australia. In America, the use of the branding iron dates back to the days when cattle roamed freely. Then, in 1867, great changes were foreshadowed by the granting of the first patent for barbed wire. Over four hundred patents for barbed wire were issued in the twenty years following 1867. Many of these patents were never followed up with actual manufacture of the wire.

The fencing-off of the land with barbed-wire fences was so hated by some of the men of the West that the Fence Wars resulted. Fences were cut illegally, blood was spilled, and enmity ruled the land. There were also a great many lawsuits over barbed wire in the early period of its history. Litigation over barbed wire lasted from 1876 to 1892.

Two types of barbed wire that were popular toward the end of the last century and are valued today by collectors are Charles Gliddens' barbed wire, patent no. 157124, and Jacob Haish's "S" barbed wire, patent no. 167240.

The cowboys, however, did not spend all their time fighting in the Fence Wars. They did quite a lot of reading, despite the popular belief that they were virtually illiterate. Some of their books they obtained in an unusual way. Cowboys rolled their own cigarettes, and the tobacco companies gave them coupons with their tobacco. The cowboys saved the coupons, sent them in, and in return they received books. Today these books are collectors' items.

Books written about the Old West are also valuable to collectors, if they are old and in good condition. Some desired titles follow:

Armstrong, **The Outlaws**
Barrett, S. M., **Geronimo's Story**
Brewerton, Lt. George D., **Overland with Kit Carson**
Collins, John S., **Across the Plains in '64**
Harman, S. W., **Hell on the Border**
Helm, Mrs. Mary S., **Scraps of Early Texas History**
McCulley, **Rangeland Justice**
Moore, **Early Cattle Days in Wyoming**
Nepton, **Over the Santa Fe Trail**
Porter, Mrs. Lavinia H., **By Ox Team to California**
Ridings, Sam P., **The Chisholm Trail**

Valued by collectors are the newspapers of the Old West, which were printed on presses brought into the new country over bad roads and despite great hardships. In these pioneer newspapers the story of the West unfolds before us as though it were happening today.

Many items are mentioned in these newspapers that were commonplace in that day but are historical curiosities in ours. One item often in the news was the Bowie knife. The original Bowie knife was designed by James Bowie, and for over sixty years his knife was one of America's favorite implements both in war and in peacetime.

War use of a Bowie knife raises its value, provided such use can be authenticated. This is especially true of those knives used in the Civil War, although Bowie knives date back to the 1830's and even to before that time. Bowie knives are still being made today, but the newer ones are not, of course, collectors' items in the true sense, and any real collector can tell them from the old ones at a glance.

The most valuable of the old knives are those with mottoes engraved on their blades, such as I DIG GOLD and DEATH TO ABOLITION. An animal's head made of silver was occasionally added to the handle of a Bowie knife, and this, too, increases the value of the knife. Although we think of the Bowie knife as being primarily American, many of the early Bowie knives were made in Sheffield, England. American firms sometimes added their own names to these knives.

Any gun authenticated as having once belonged to an outlaw, especially a famous outlaw, has value. Relics such as scalps, hanging ropes, the records of old trials and lynchings, jail keys, "Wanted" posters and other mementoes of the outlaws are desired.

Sheriffs' badges from the Old West also have value, but, again, they must be authenticated. It always helps if it can be proved that a badge had been worn by a famous U.S. marshal or sheriff.

The trails to the West may still yield treasure. Mementoes of the Oregon Trail, the Santa Fe Trail, the California Cut-off, the Spanish Trail and the Chisholm Trail are highly desired by the collectors.

Documents, books or any kind of records of the West are important and valuable. One document, signed by an early Indian scout named Croghan, was recently sold for four hundred dollars.

Another kind of record that has come down to us from the days of the pioneers is the work of Charles Russell. Russell was one of the finest painters of the Old West; he had worked as a ranch hand and knew intimately the scenes that he painted. It has been estimated that Russell executed more than three thousand works of art during his lifetime, including some sculptured bronzes. Many of his paintings have never been reproduced. Authentic Russells (with the Russell monogram) are prized by museums and collectors.

The frontiersmen's wives and mothers brought along many household and personal items from their homes in the East when they accompanied their men into the new land. Any of these items used by the frontier women would have value today: kettles and cooking equipment, clothing, "heirlooms" of all kinds, bedding, cradles and other furniture, and such things as brooms made of branches that were made for them by their menfolk, hand-whittled butter paddles, dippers and cups. The dishes that went west with the wagon trains were made of tin; what good dishes the families owned were of necessity packed away and were not used on the long journey.

Our pioneers were a hardy and enduring people. They turned a wilderness into a civilized land. They left behind them their relics and records, each item telling a new and different tale of our lost but legendary West.

XV

MISSING PAINTINGS AND A DISAPPEARING ARTIST

Lost Works of American Artists

IF you visit the National Gallery of Art in Washington, D.C., you will see there a painting called "The Lackawanna Valley" by George Inness, one of our most famous American painters.

In the 1800's, George D. Phelps, first president of the Delaware and Lackawanna Railroad, decided it would be a good idea to have a painting of the railroad's first roundhouse. Phelps also decided that the painter for the job was George Inness and that the picture should be used for advertising purposes.

Inness consented and set out by stagecoach to reach the round-house—a rather unpleasant journey, especially since he managed to lose all his luggage and had to write home for funds to keep going.

Yet he did arrive, executed the painting and showed it to the railroad committee. These gentlemen, however, instead of praising the painting, protested angrily because Inness had not portrayed all four of the trains the railroad owned.

Inness went back and put in the four trains, at least theoretically—because he needed the seventy-five dollars the railroad had promised him for the work. He also put in the initials D. L. & W. on the tender of the first locomotive, as the committee demanded, although the request irritated him. He got back at the committee in his own way, however: the only evidence of the fourth train in the painting is the smoke from its locomotive.

This painting has not always been at the National Gallery, however. As a matter of fact, it was lost for thirty years. Then an amazing thing happened. Paintings have been lost and then found before— but this is the only occasion I ever heard of where the painter of the missing picture found his own work.

Some time in the 1880's, Inness went to Mexico City. Browsing in a junk shop one day, he spotted "The Lackawanna Valley," part of a job lot of office furnishings that had been purchased by the proprietor. Inness bought it back, thus claiming for himself the unusual distinction of finding a lost treasure that he himself had created.

SOMEDAY perhaps the largest painting in the world, or at least some pieces of it, may be found in a junk shop, the way the Inness painting was found. This is the Banvard panorama, which is regarded by some as the largest painting ever executed. Entitled "The Panorama of the Mississippi," it is a view of the Mississippi River and its scenery.

It was in 1840 that John Banvard traveled from St. Louis down the Mississippi to begin his work. During his journey, Banvard made hundreds of preliminary sketches, covering twelve hundred miles of scenery. Eventually the sketches were joined together to form one long, continuous panorama. It was mounted between rollers, and was usually exhibited on a stage.

According to Banvard's publicity, the painting showed three thousand miles of scenery, and could be stretched out to a length of three miles. The painting was probably nowhere near that big, however, and it probably showed far less than three thousand miles of scenery. Yet, whatever the size actually was, the Banvard painting may still be regarded as one of the largest in the world, if not the very largest.

I cannot imagine how anyone could possibly lose something of the size of the Banvard panorama, but it happened. It is now lost. One authority seems to feel that portions of this painting were left abroad, while other portions were brought back to this country by Banvard. Another authority claims that the panorama was lost in India, after being purchased by an Englishman.

There is a theory that the Banvard canvas may have been cut up to be used for theatrical backdrops. Even if this is so, the pieces, if found and authenticated, would have value.

We are quite certain as to what the painting looked like, since there were advertisements for it, as well as guide books that described the panorama in detail; and some of these ads and guide books are still in existence.

Panoramas like Banvard's were a vogue for awhile in America. Sometimes the canvases for the panoramas were ten feet high, and a speaker would explain the panorama as it unrolled. One of the panoramas that is still in existence is "The Panorama of a Whaling Voyage Around the World," executed by Benjamin Russell and Caleb Purrington. Over a thousand feet long and over eight feet high, the "Whaling Voyage" is today on view at the Old Dartmouth Historical Society and Whaling Museum in New Bedford, Mass.

When the Banvard panorama was shown in America, a poet sat in the audience, not one night, but night after night. He seemed especially interested in the portion of the panorama that showed Louisiana.

From his seat he watched intently as view after view of the Louisiana country was unrolled. From these viewings of Banvard's panorama came the descriptions for a poem he was writing.

The poem? *Evangeline!*

The poet? Henry Wadsworth Longfellow!

THOMAS Chambers, one of America's so-called Primitive artists, disappeared over a century ago. Yet only a few years ago, paintings done in his style were discovered in California.

Artists like Chambers were the amateurs of their day. They produced an art that was strictly nonprofessional in quality. Today we call such art American Primitive. Primitive art can be anything done by an amateur but representative of our culture for a particular period in America's past. This can be anything from a chalk drawing on a piece of scratch paper to a painting that is almost traditional in scope and esthetic concept.

The subject matter can be almost anything, a portrait, seascapes, the life around the artist, the artist's conception of historical events as he heard about them or in rare cases as he witnessed them. Even badly done family portraits can be valuable at times, if not for their artistic value then for historical and sentimental reasons.

Some of these amateur paintings were done by men who did manage to make their living at it. They would go so far toward mass production, in some cases, that they would carry around paintings of people with only the features left out. Then when they found a customer, they filled in the face.

To give a list of Primitive artists to watch for would be almost ridiculous, since most of them are unknown. Usually an American Primitive painting will be signed by someone no one ever heard of.

Just such an artist was Thomas Chambers, who lived in the 1800's and who was not considered a great artist by the experts of his own day, let alone by the experts of today. As a matter of fact, he was thought of more as a sign painter than as a fine artist, at least according to one authority.

Chambers' works are usually concerned with rivers, river life and water. He did paintings of the Hudson Valley as well as paintings of the sea. One of his most interesting *known* paintings is "The Constitution and the Guerrière."

There are today approximately twenty-four pictures absolutely identified as being by the hand of Thomas Chambers. Others are of doubtful authenticity, one reason being that so little is known of either Chambers or his life. It would be possible to check out at least part of his life, since his name appears in very old Boston and New York directories, yet he was not listed in the catalogs of the various art exhibitions of his day.

Chambers disappeared from sight some time during the 1850's. One theory concerning his disappearance is that he rushed to California with the rest of the hopefuls when the full impact of the Gold Rush hit that state.

Chambers' paintings could now be found anywhere, but for obvious reasons California would be the best place to start looking for any works he may have executed in the latter part of his life; indeed, paintings in Chambers' style have already been found there.

I wonder if perhaps some of the Chambers California paintings that are still lost might not depict the streams and rivers of California where the prospectors worked and dreamed of gold.

Anything is possible. More Chambers paintings might still be found, perhaps in the same manner as certain paintings by Charles

Willson Peale were found, which had been on the missing list for over a century and a half.

In the late 1700's, two of Peale's paintings, one of George Washington and one of General Nathaniel Greene, were taken from America to Great Britain. Then they disappeared and were missing for over a century and a half.

Imagine the disbelief on the face of the individual who finally located the Peale portraits! They were in the attic of a home in England, well hidden from prying eyes until the day when someone did see them and recognized them for what they were.

So, too, paintings by Thomas Chambers might very well be hidden in an attic or a junk store or in the city dump.

XVI

FOR THE GLORY OF GOD

Religious Treasures

WHEN the tomb of the great King Charlemagne was opened in the twelfth century, he was found sitting upright, completely attired in his imperial regalia like a ghost sovereign holding sway over an empire of dust and decay.

But the emperor was not the only thing they found, for in his tomb they discovered a fabulous reliquary, set with sapphires and allegedly containing a piece of the "true cross." The reliquary had rested there quietly for centuries, until 1804, when one of the most beautiful women in Europe visited the tomb at Aix-la-Chapelle. Joséphine de Beauharnais took one look at the reliquary and wanted it.

There was consternation among the treasure keepers of the tomb, but Napoléon Bonaparte insisted and, reluctantly, the keepers gave the reliquary to Joséphine. Where this reliquary is today is a mystery, although rumor has it that it is now in the hands of a French collector. If this is true then it does not belong on the treasure hunter's list. But there were other reliquaries made by the order of Charlemagne which really belong on the treasure hunter's list—for they are missing, completely lost to the world.

Among them are the twenty-four alphabet reliquaries, each of them encrusted with precious gems and each designed for a different letter of the alphabet. The last trace we have of these reliquaries

88

is in the eleventh century, when the so-called "A of Charlemagne," the first of the reliquaries, belonged to a Church in Conques.

Since then, there is no trace of them, and not even the Vatican has any knowledge of the letters. Tiffany's in New York relegates them to the world of legend. Gump's in San Francisco has no information on them. Nor does the College of St. Albert the Great, Dominican House of Studies for the Province of the Holy Name, in Oakland, have any information.

They have become lost even to the historians, but, if you could find even one of the letters, it would be listed as one of the greatest religious treasures found in the last century. They could be anywhere —even in your attic here in America—for when the priests came to this country they brought with them as many of their treasures as they could.

It would not be incredible at all to find one of these reliquaries decorating the altar of some small church in one of America's backwaters. Or one may be in that old trunk in your basement which contains the souvenirs of an ancestor who had been to sea and collected many strange things in even stranger ports.

Or, perhaps, you might find a different reliquary there—even though it might not be one of the twenty-four reliquaries of Charlemagne. Numerous reliquaries were made in the time of the early Christian church, reliquaries made with loving care and decorated with the most costly materials and gems which the artisans could find. For these were the caskets which contained the relics of their saints—sometimes a bone or a fingernail or a piece of hair. Or sometimes even a piece of wood which was allegedly a piece of the "true cross."

These reliquaries were made in many forms, and one of these forms was that of a cross. Since these altar reliquaries were made to hold the relics of their saints, the churches made them with the finest workmanship and costliest gems—each of them a treasure—if you could find it.

There are, of course, reliquaries in the museums today, but there were so many made that there is no way of knowing, since the records are so vague, how many are missing. It is simpler to remember just what reliquaries are and to watch for them.

Remember also that there are so many objects in the world of religion to watch for, because it was here, in the church, where people poured out their hopes and dreams—and in so doing produced some of the world's most beautiful art.

Specialized works of art were also produced, eagerly desired by collectors. From twelfth-century Byzantine art, watch for the Black Virgins: art representing the Virgin Mary with her skin painted black to show her sorrow.

The color black, though again associated with lost religious treasures, is not always associated with sorrow. From the Middle ages watch for representations of Jesus clothed in black garments. Black in this case means death—death to evil. How many of these black Virgins or black Christs were made, or how many are missing, no one knows. One thing, however, is certain: they will be bought by museums—if you can find them.

They could be anywhere. Treasures travel to fantastic places— sometimes right under your nose if you only know what you are looking for. It is to be hoped, of course, that, if you should find a lost religious treasure, it would be in fine condition, for this is important in evaluating any item.

This demand for fine condition also holds true for the wax figures of the saints made during the feudal ages—if you can find them. It also holds true for the stained-glass windows of Europe which even in the tenth century were used to beautify the houses of God.

Stained-glass windows previous to the twelfth century were brilliant in their colors, but by the twelfth century the monks of the Cistercian order issued proclamations to the effect that the violent color of the windows must be subdued.

This edict greatly influenced the creation of stained-glass windows throughout all of Europe, and, in the fourteenth century, there was another stoppage to the making of fine stained-glass windows. This was that medieval phenomenon which was rightly called the Black Death.

The somber churches of the Middle Ages with their vastness and their feeling of immensity possibly needed the glory and brilliancy that comes from a sunbeam slanting through the rich purples and violets of these paintings done in glass.

Any of these fabled windows from any of these centuries is worth watching for, and while there may be little chance of finding a piece or a whole portion of a stained-glass window, still the treasures are there to be found. What museum would not want a fine rainbow-hued window from the Middle Ages?

Think it impossible to find a stained-glass window in America? What, then, of the millionaire California gold-rush miners who shipped treasure here by the wagonload—and then lost it. Or the show-off business tycoons of the '20's who bought treasure by the boatload when most of them did not even know art when they saw it. And many lost it after the crash of '29. Even a stained-glass window could be anywhere in America—if you only bother to look for it. And if you find a religious treasure—of fine craftsmanship and in fine condition—you have something which collectors and museum curators will pay for.

TO the experts a bulto means a carved figure or a figure representing the Madonna, the Christ or the Saints. To the experts a retablo means a religious painting done on wood or skin. To the experts these are examples of very primitive art done in the lands south of the border by the peons. But to the treasure hunter they are lost treasures well worth searching for.

It all began when the conquistadores marched with heavy feet across the lands to the south of us, and the priests of the church went with them. The spilling of blood and the awareness of a new kind of God walked hand in hand.

As early as the fifteen hundreds, the people were helping to decorate their churches. The works of art which they created are to all purposes the art of the people themselves. No Raphaels or da Vincis here, but poor, uneducated people with a need to display their great love for their Church.

Many of these unknown artists were Indians, sometimes of mixed blood, and it was to these people that the Church looked for much of its art. Their works were simple, yet filled with the grandeur of their beliefs. They, from all parts of the Latin countries in our hemisphere, created works of art for the missions, the churches, the schools.

There was no building of religious significance which they did not beautify in some way. No matter how poor the people were, they glorified the Church. They spilled what wealth they had into its paintings, its statues and its decorations. They made bultos and retablos, altar pieces, wood panels, and crucifixes.

Part of this art has survived. Much has disappeared and may today lie forgotten in some peon's hut or even in the home of some American who traveled into the lands of the south and purchased some items from the "natives." Not knowing the value of what they had, it is possible that the peons sold for pennies objects which are actually very valuable. The Americans in their turn bought what they thought were oddities, never dreaming that they were buying works of art which belong in the museums.

How many of these works of art have survived at all is unknown. Some of them of course have been damaged. In the many revolutions which have rocked the southern nations numerous works of art were used as parts of tents, or the paintings were placed so that they gave shade to the tired soldiers. Some of the art was ruthlessly destroyed by soldiers in their revolutionary desire for destruction. Some was simply thrown away by revolutionaries who wanted something new and who looked down upon the primitive art of their own country. Many times some fine art was thrown on the junk heap while paintings and statues of far less beauty and merit were put in its place.

Sometimes they were simply put away, out of sight, because they were misunderstood and not appreciated properly. Some of them might still be found in the dark corners of Latin America, where they have lain waiting for someone who knows their value to claim them.

What is the value of these items? Whatever the market will bear —depending upon the object's condition, the workmanship and the desire of the buyer.

Where to find them? In all of the countries to the south which knew the influence of the Church. Mexico is especially considered to be one of the finest hunting grounds for the art of these primitive artisans.

Perhaps the bulto or retablo or crucifix which you picked up on your vacation in Mexico might be one that satisfies the demands of the collectors in terms of beauty, workmanship, and age. So many of these primitive works of art have disappeared that your chances for finding one of them are very good.

XVII

WHODUNIT?

Clues to Famous Mysteries

COULD you solve a famous mystery? Everyone would like to think they could!

You could, as the saying goes, write your own ticket if you could find the answers to any one of a number of famous mysteries. You would, of course, have to provide proof—real, authentic proof that could not now, or ever, be doubted. Proof that would provide complete, accurate and indisputable answers!

For example: What really happened to Jesse James? Was he really killed by Bob Ford, or was that a double, and did Jesse escape back to the West? Was that really Hitler's body that was burned in the bunker, or did he escape in a submarine, as has been said so often? What really happened to Amelia Earhart? Was she a victim of the Japanese, did she die in the ocean, or is she still on some Pacific Island watching the skies for the rescue that never comes? Was Mary Queen of Scots really guilty of the murder of her husband, Lord Darnley, as so many historians have thought? Or was she an innocent victim of circumstance?

Who was Kasper Hauser, the man who, not too many years ago, appeared in Europe? To all intents and purposes he came from nowhere and he knew nothing, of either languages, manners or customs, of those around him. Even today there are people who write and wonder about Kasper Hauser, who he was and where he came from.

What happened to the members of the lost colony, those colonists who came to America and disappeared some time between 1587 and 1590? It is assumed that they intermarried with the Indians, but this has never been proven.

Who were the Cagots? Were they lepers, cannibals, or descendants of the Saracens? Today, no one knows. We know only that they lived during the Middle Ages in the south of France, and that they were so abhorred that no one would walk on the same side of the street with them; special holy water fonts were placed in the churches for them; and their feet were bored with an iron. Even today the word Cagot is used to frighten French children, but who they were or why they were so despised is unknown.

Do you know the true identity of the man in the iron mask? This man actually existed and was not just a figment of the imaginations of mystery writers. The mask he wore was of black velvet, however.

He was a prisoner in several different prisons in France during the reign of Louis XIV, and he wore his mask until the day of his death when he was buried in France, his identity as unknown then as it is today.

When he died, he was placed in his grave under the name of Marchioli, yet this was not his name. Writers have argued that he was a twin brother of a French king; that he was the Duke of Monmouth; and that he was Fouquet. None of these suggestions nor the many other suggestions that followed his death have been either proven or disproven.

And sometimes, there are those mysterious disappearances that might provide a rapid reward if you could solve them. Every year hundreds of people disappear, and almost all of them have families or friends who want them back: husbands, wives, children, relatives of all kinds.

Witnesses to accidents or legal papers have disappeared, many times not even knowing they are wanted. And sometimes there are cases of amnesia, about which there have been so many stories written.

In many if not all of these cases the families are willing to pay at least a token reward and sometimes, if the families are wealthy, a fantastic remuneration.

What happened to Judge Crater? No one knows but everyone

would like to know what happened to him. Magazines, newspapers, any medium of communication would welcome the opportunity of filling the pockets of the man who could find accurate verifiable information as to what really happened to this most famous of all missing persons.

Ambrose Bierce, the man who wrote stories of mysterious disappearances, himself disappeared into Mexico in 1914 and was never heard from again. Strangely enough, he had told friends that he had a premonition of his death shortly before this.

And there are other mysteries that are well worth looking into, mysteries which are still considered completely or partially unsolved. This is true of information, verifiable of course, on any of the famous killers or murder trials of the past. Something new on the Barbara Graham case, the Caryl Chessman case or the guilt or innocence of Dr. Mudd would be very valuable to you if you found the right market for it, such as newspapers, magazines, or any news media.

Other than this market, there is always the chance that some of the rewards that were offered by the public might still be available. Possibly not, but you could still name your own price to any of the media which deal in crime, the history of crime, or just plain sensationalism.

Also, watch for the collectible relics of such famous killers as Johann Schneider, who put his victim's body in a bake-house oven; Kemmler, the first man to be electrocuted; or Mrs. Pearcey, who put the bodies of her victims, a mother and child, in a baby buggy and wheeled them about the streets of London.

If the items you find or the information you locate relate to a wanted criminal, then the idea of being able to collect a reward is a good one, providing you keep in mind that most of these rewards are offered by private parties, private groups, interested parties, etc. The FBI, for example does not have funds which can be used for reward purposes.

Local organizations, many times, offer rewards, and it is to the advantage of the citizen to look into this, if and when he or she does manage to obtain information on missing criminals. The first steps, of course, would be to obtain the information, then pass it along to the police. Then ask about rewards. The police themselves may not have offered the reward or even have it available, but they will know who did.

Sometimes no official reward is ever offered—not matter how famous the crime or the criminal. For example, no official reward was ever offered for the solution of one of the most horrible series of crimes ever committed, but if you could offer any kind of proof as to the true identity of Jack the Ripper, magazines, newspaper, any kind of news media would settle for almost any price you cared to name for your information, your diaries, letters, whatever it is you happen to have found.

It has been many years since the Ripper stalked the streets of London, yet his crimes are as alive and as gruesome today as on August 7, 1888, when he destroyed and mutilated his first victim.

A theory held by many of those who have read about and discussed the Jack the Ripper case for many years is that he knew the girls he killed. This is said because, following the first atrocities, Whitechapel was filled with policemen. Guards were stationed, girls were warned, every inch of ground was gone over again and again, and yet, even with the police on every side of him, the Ripper struck again and again and again.

Because of this, it was felt that he had to be a man the girls knew or they would not have let him get within ten feet of them on the nights when all of London knew that Jack the Ripper stalked the streets of Whitechapel.

It is this theory that lays the case of Jack the Ripper open to the hopes of the treasure hunter, because if the Ripper did know these girls, then somewhere along the line one of them must have mentioned him—in a diary or in a note to a friend, and if they did and you find it, it might lead to the discovery of who the Ripper really was. Naturally, she would not have called him Jack the Ripper, because until the moment when he killed her she must have known him only as an acquaintance or as a friend. Rather, he would have been mentioned by a name unrecognizable as one being synonymous with Jack the Ripper; but mention of a man the girl knew, a man she had hurt, a man she was angry with or who himself was angry with all women, might be enough to lead the experts to a true identification, even after all these years.

Letters, diaries, or notes signed by the following girls and dated before the dates listed, since these dates were the last days of their lives, might finally solve the case of Jack the Ripper. On the days

mentioned they met for the last time, at the places stated, the gentleman we call Jack the Ripper.

Martha Tabran or **Turner**
   August 7, 1888, George Yard Buildings, Whitechapel
Mary Ann Nichols
   August 31, 1888, Bucks Row, Whitechapel
Annie Chapman
   September 8, 1888, Hanbury Street, Whitechapel
Elizabeth Stride
   September 30, 1888, Berners Street, Whitechapel
Catherine Eddowes
   September 30, 1888, Mitre Square, Whitechapel
Marie Jeanette Kelly
   November 9, 1888, Dorset Street, Whitechapel
Alice McKenzie
   July 17, 1889, Castle Alley, Whitechapel

Because of all the similarities between the killings, as you can see
in the list above, the fact that all the murders happened in Whitechapel and the fact that all of them were mutilated in a similar manner with the exception of one girl, many people believe that the girls
in question were all killed by the same man, a man who used his
knife as only a doctor or a butcher could have done. That's why they
call him Jack the Ripper.

If you could locate mementoes, curios, diaries, letters, or anything
that could provide the final clue to prove the true identity of Jack the
Ripper, you could name your own price—from any news media.

Many, many strange things from the dark world of courtrooms,
dungeons, prisons and gallows are collectible items. Any article of
punishment or torture ranks as a collectors' item. The scourges, flesh-
tearing hooks, racks, even old handcuffs and leg irons are gruesome
and valuable reminders of the justice of a by-gone day.

There is a kind of shirt, rather long, painted with all kinds of signs,
symbols, and the names of various crimes. These were the so-called
San Benitos, those garments that were worn by those condemned to
death in the Inquisition.

If you should happen to find a very large barrel with strange holes
in it, you may have found a collectors' item. It should be old enough
to have been made in the 1600's; it should have one large hole in the
top for a man's head, a hole on each side for a man's arms, and two
holes in the bottom for a man's legs. Such barrels as these were used
in England as a means of punishment for drunkards. The inebriated

offender was placed inside the barrel to serve out his sentence, little realizing as he did so that the wooden atrocity around him would someday be considered an item of value to the collector.

Relics of the gypsies of the Middle Ages come within the realm of the collectors of gruesome objects if they are items connected with any of the various crimes for which the gypsies were persecuted during all the centuries of the Dark Ages.

The old bell, which at one time rang out for criminals from England's Newgate Prison on their way to be hanged, was saved from destruction in 1903, when it was purchased and placed in Madame Tussaud's Chamber of Horrors in London. Newgate itself fell at the hands of wrecking experts in 1903 but the bell itself survived, an awesome reminder of the more gruesome aspects of another age.

Keys of famous prisons are also collectors' items. The key to the most famous of the older prisons, the Bastille, is now at Mount Vernon. It was given to Washington by LaFayette.

Thousands of Frenchmen died under the blood-soaked blade of the guillotine during the days of the French Revolution. The knife itself from this instrument of murder is now a part of Madame Tussaud's Exhibition in London. This is all that is left of the entire guillotine, which was destroyed in the 1925 fire at Madame Tussaud's, yet even the knife itself is looked upon as an important remnant of a memento of France's revolution.

Yet there was a time when the guillotine stood outside a pawnshop and no-one wanted it. It might have been lost completely to historians if the original owner, executioner Clement Henri Sanson, had not offered it for sale to Tussaud's.

Mementoes of the famous executioners of the past are collectors' items. Such men as Richard Brandon, who was supposed to have executed Charles I; Jack Ketch, who allegedly executed the Duke of Monmouth, but who was so nervous about it that he had to use the axe five times and then use a knife to cut the head from the body. Relics of Bulle, who executed Mary Queen of Scots, have value.

Even relics of witchcraft have value. Witchcraft is not a new thing. It is an ancient and evil art, and sometimes, if the treasure hunter is lucky enough, some of the mementoes of the necromancers and the sorcerers are still to be found.

Watch for witch figures, those figures made of clay and impregnated with fingernail clippings, hair and spit of the victim, which are collectors' items. Yet it is wise to remember that there are several different figures of this type. They were made in a similar fashion and for the same purposes but some are those of the Dark Ages in Europe, some are from Colonial America and some are Indian, pre-dating even the landings of Columbus.

Have you ever seen the autograph of a witch? If you have, you have seen a collectors' item. The original records of the Salem witch trials can be seen by the public at the Office of Clerk of the Courts in Salem, Mass. The same office also displays the pins that the victims of the witches were allegedly pricked with.

The witch trials of Salem make up a fascinating portion of our history, but because of their nature, most of the records of the alleged witchcraft have not been preserved. Yet, there still may be diaries or letters of these so-called witches, telling of their emotions or their fears and the last desperate struggles against the prejudices of their age. Watch for any note, memo, letters or diaries belonging to:

> Bridget Bishop
> Sarah Good
> Sarah Wilds
> Elizabeth Howe
> Susanna Martin
> Rebecca Nourse
> George Burroughs
> John Proctor
> George Jacobs, Sr.
> John Willard
> Martha Carrier
> Martha Corey
> Mary Easty
> Alice Parker
> Ann Pudeator
> Margaret Scott
> Wilmot Reed
> Samuel Wardwell
> Mary Parker
> Giles Corey

From mysteries to murder to witchcraft—everything has value, if you can recognize it when you find it.

XVIII

THE CHILDREN'S HOUR

Childhood Treasures

IN the search for lost treasures of all kinds, not even such a mundane item as the "potty chair" should be overlooked. Potty chairs of the early 1700's actually belong in the museums—and not in your attic or basement.

Shaped like miniature wing chairs with a hole cut in the seat, they may differ a little in design from our modern potty chairs but certainly no one can mistake them for anything else but what they are.

Even potty chairs from a later period, the early 1800's, are worth rescuing from the junk pile, since they can be valued at around $50 apiece, making them worth what little trouble it takes to cart them down from the attic.

Anything the young ones of long ago needed is worth locating. Like the objects made for infants who reached the crawling stage, for among these are the early Colonial "fenders," which were built to keep the little ones from burning themselves in the fireplace.

Or the ladder-back high chairs of the late 1700's. One of these is today on display in Pilgrim Hall, Plymouth, Mass., and if you are lucky enough, you might find another similar to it.

Children's cradles from the Colonial period are items eagerly sought by collectors. Condition and age, of course, are important here, but it is still possible to find them occasionally.

Even the old-fashioned "baby tenders" dating from the 1700's are collectors' items. These were standing stools made complete with a tray for the child's toys.

And then, of course, there are always the "hornbooks!" When America was young, times were very different. Paper was scarce and education was limited. Yet one thing, however, was then as it is today: the general contrariness and destructiveness of the younger generation.

Still, the young ones had to be taught, so the older generation made use of an "elementary school book." This was a "book" which had been used previously in older countries and which is generally called a "hornbook."

The American hornbook consisted of one sheet, on which was printed the alphabet and the Lord's Prayer. To save the sheet, which was considered very precious, it was pasted upon wood and then covered with a thin, transparent piece of horn; thus the name hornbook.

Occasionally there were other items on the page besides the alphabet and the Prayer. There were Roman numerals, capital letters or syllables, and sometimes arithmetic and religious instructions. The page always listed the alphabet in one form or another, and for this reason gained another name: the "abcderia."

Thousands of these abcderias were made in America, yet only very few have ever been located. This is one reason why they are considered collectors' items.

They are also important to us because from them our first Americans learned their daily lessons. However, much to the chagrin of these boys and girls of another day, the hornbook could and was put to an entirely different purpose. The hornbooks were made in the shape of paddles and when the young student did not learn his lesson properly, he was upended and his hornbook used to impress him with the necessity for doing better on the following day.

It must have seemed incongruous to the young student that his hornbook was considered so valuable that he was not allowed to touch it even while studying, but his elders could, and did, use it, of all things, as a paddle.

Of course, not every children's item which you should watch for were so disliked by them. Toys headed the children's list of enjoyable items—and they should be at the top of the treasure hunter's list of odds and ends he might find anywhere, from his attic to his cellar.

Like the toy fire engines made during the 1800's which are now valued at close to $100 apiece. Or toy strollers, the old fashioned wicker kind which you see occasionally at auctions, and which may be valued at $25 or $30, depending on age and condition.

Also, do not forget the trading cards, which were originally put out as part of an advertising scheme. These were the advertisers' commercials of the gay nineties. They were comical or had colorful puzzles on them, or sometimes even pretty girls—all with the purpose of selling something to the consumer.

The children collected them then, as now they collect airplane and baseball cards. Today, these trading cards of yesteryear belong in the hands of the collectors. Value of these cards depends of course on their rarity and condition, but, if you can find a rare example in fine condition, the collectors will buy it eagerly.

Early Colonial or early American toys of any kind are all worth something. It has not been a hundred years since the manufacture of toys became widespread in America. Early toys were made without the benefits of mass production, and because of this they were expensive. Because of this they are also extremely rare and valuable —if you can find them.

This scarcity of toys is not only true of early Colonial toys. It is also true of all the ages before this time, and this is a fact which you must remember when watching for toys.

Toys in Early America were scarce—and dear to the children. Some of the toys were quite old and may even have been brought from Europe by the first pioneers, perhaps even drawn across country in the covered wagons.

Who knows, for instance, in what backwoods second-hand store you might find toys dating back to the times of the Middle Ages! These European toys were often of the finest quality, some of them having been made by the same master goldsmiths who made jewelry and ornaments for the finest gentry. Little toy knights and toy flags with which the children played "crusader."

Sometimes an item from an earlier period than our own might, to our eyes, resemble toys—and yet not have been used as toys at all! Like the fashion dolls which members of European royal families sent to each other, and the Parisian fashion dolls which were set up on display in Europe. Dressed in the rich, luxurious clothing of their times, these fashion dolls of the Middle Ages are today collectors' items. Two dolls of this type are today on display at the University of Upsala in Sweden.

Even in a later period, fashion dolls made to display fashions of the period were popular. Colonial fashion dolls are also collectors' items. Some of them were brought to this country directly from France during the pre-Revolutionary days.

Yet in Colonial days fashion was not the only thing in the minds of the mothers, and dolls were also for the children to play with. Watch for any doll that is this old. You should even investigate hand-whittled wooden dolls for their possible value, as well as any of the cornhusk dolls you might find. These were crude, simple creations made from cornhusks by both the pioneers and the Indians.

There was not even one doll factory in the United States until the late 1800's; dolls were either imported or made by friends or parents. Any of these dolls is worth investigating. German dolls were imported to America for many, many years. These lovely old dolls came all the way from Germany to gladden the hearts of American children. Some had blue eyes, and they are the rarest—and the ones that should be watched for.

Also look for dolls which were made of a combination of wood and pewter. These can be valued at around $80 apiece, if they are old enough, in fine enough condition—and if you can find them.

Also watch for old dolls with china heads. They, too, have become collector's items. Watch for costume dolls. Some of these are quite rare and unusual, and certainly well worth investigating if they are old enough.

Also watch for doll houses, some of which are very old and quite fabulous and, as such, are collectors' items. Complete with dolls, rugs and everything else a real home would have, they belong in the museums—if you can find them. Some of the European doll houses were not made for the children, however, but for the adults. They were large doll houses, sometimes eight feet high, and a few are today in museums in Europe—where you could place another if you could find it.

Most of the doll houses, however, were made for the children, as were the toys, furniture and dolls, but whatever it is, if it belonged to a child and if it is rare enough, old enough and in fine enough condition, the collectors will pay you well for it—if you can find it.

ALL parents who want their children to save money buy banks for them. Or at least that is the way it used to be. Today, it is the parents who want the old banks because they can be lost treasures in disguise.

There are mechanical, semi-mechanical and still banks—all of them worth at least something. Some of them are worth a great deal, depending upon rarity, condition, and age.

There is, of course, no way of telling exactly which banks are missing. What we do have is a series of values for known banks that have passed into or through the hands of the experts—and if you are lucky, you will find similar ones. Or possibly you might even find a very rare bank that has never even been listed.

Values for some of the more valuable known mechanical, semi-mechanical and still banks are as follows:

> **Afghanistan**—$300-$400.
> **"American Bank" sewing machine**—$400.
> **Aunt Dinah and The Good Fairy**—$450.
>
> **Billy Goat**—$350-$450.
> **Bowling Alley**—$550.
> **Bread Winners Bank**—$350-$400.
> **Building, Cupola and Man**—$400.
> **Bull and Bear**—$200-$600.
> **Bull**—[Charges, tosses boy into well, made of brass] $450-$850.
>
> **Called Out**—$400-$850.
> **Camera**—$500-$1,000.
> **Cannon**—[Shooting into octagonal fort] $300-$500.
> **Cat**—[Jumps for mouse] $400.
> **Circus**—$600-$1,000.
> **Confectionary**—$450-$700.
>
> **Ferris Wheel**—$450.
> **Fort**—[Octagonal] $400.
> **Fortune Teller**—["Drop a coin and I will tell your fortune"] $500.
> **Fortune Teller**—[Safe] $400.
> **Fowler**—$450-$650.
> **Freedman's Bank**—[Wood, cloth and white metal, metal clockwork] $650.
>
> **Giant**—$300-$900.
> **Girl in Victorian Chair**—$325-$750.
> **Girl Skipping Rope**—$550-$800.

Goat, Frog and Old Man—$400-$500.
Grenadier—$200.

Help the Blind—$500.

Initiating—$350-$850.

Katzenjammer—$275-$500.

Locomotive—[Fireman shovels coin into firebox] $500.

Man—[In frock coat, behind grill] $400.
Mikado—$600-$1500.
Motor Bank—$450.

North Pole—$500-$900.
Novelty—["Johnson's Patent"] $400.

Old Woman Who Lived in a Shoe—$600.

Panorama—$300-$400.
Patronize the Blind Man—$400.
Perfection Registering Bank—$500.
Picture Gallery—$200-$500.
Preacher in Pulpit—$400.
Presto—[Mouse comes out of roof] $450.

Ram—[Bucking, boy thumbs nose] $350-$500.
Red Riding Hood—$600.

Shoot the Chute—$500-$1200.

Teddy and The Bear—$75.
Turtle—$400.

Uncle Remus—$450-$600.

Wishbone—$500.
Woman in Shoe—$600.
Woodpecker—[Tree trunk, musical, foreign] $400.

Watch for any of the above. That old bank made to save pennies might turn out to be worth many dollars.

XIX

MONEY, MONEY EVERYWHERE

Nickels, Half-Dollars and Dollars

EVERY day you see at least one buffalo nickel—and use it to buy a nickel's worth of gum or pencils or candy. But you ought to look at it more carefully before you spend it, because if it happens to be a 1937 buffalo nickel issued by the Denver mint, *and* if the buffalo has only three legs, then the nickel is worth as much as $125.

So recent yet so valuable—in direct opposition to the popular conception of the value of coins. And one of the most costly mistakes a person looking for rare coins can make is to think that age is a primary factor in determining value.

Coins of ancient Rome, for example, are sometimes worth as little as fifty cents, and some recent coins, such as the above nickel, are worth small fortunes.

Other factors, also, determine the value of a coin. To be valuable a coin must be in excellent condition and be considered a rarity by the collectors. Sometimes a coin is rare because only a few are issued, such as the 1861 Confederate silver half-dollar. Only four of this type and this date were issued, and for this reason the value of this coin can go as high as $20,000. (This is not the restrike of 1879, which is only worth about $200 to $400.)

There are times when a coin is such a rarity that the collectors will pay almost any price for it. One of these is the 1804 silver dollar, so rare that collectors all over the world would bid for it—if you could find it.

Today a few examples of this rare coin have been found and placed in the hands of the collectors. Estimates of this fabled dollar have reached as high as $30,000, a three million percent profit from an investment of a dollar—if you can find one.

Not quite so profitable, yet still high on the treasure hunter's list is an "eight bit" piece which is valued as high as $15,000. This is the Brasher Doubloon, a coin struck in 1787 by Ephraim Brasher.

The Brasher Doubloon is made of gold. On one side of the coin is a mountain with a sun rising behind it, and on the other side is a spread eagle. The coin may also be identified by the punch mark, which is EB.

The Brasher Doubloon, of course, is one of those coins which for most of us automatically suggests great value. This certainly is true but, fortunately for the treasure hunter, there are other coins which should not be overlooked by the seeker of treasures.

One of these is the unc. 1914 D Lincoln cent, either one by one or by the roll. Each of these pennies—if their condition satisfies the numismatists, can be valued as high as $350. A roll of these pennies is worth up to $17,500.

Later in issue, yet still valuable, are the 1921 S Lincoln pennies, which are worth up to $125 apiece—or $6,250 for a roll of fifty.

Many coins are of some value yet not worth fortunes, such as the Massachusetts Pine, Oak, and Willow Tree coins, which are only worth from $50 to $100, or the Sommer Island Shilling, which is valued from $75 to $250. Yet I do not suppose that anyone would willingly throw away coins worth such "minor" value. Even a small return is better than none.

Markets for coins are relatively easy to find. Coin collecting is one of the most common hobbies in the world, and collectors bid eagerly for good specimens. In America alone there are over twenty-five thousand numismatists and well over 100,000 active, enthusiastic "coin collectors." There are coin shops in almost every city, every town, every village in the nation.

Finds have been made in the past and will, undoubtedly, be made again. It is far better to laboriously watch over every coin you receive than to acquire a coin worth a fortune and lose it by handing it out as change to the man at the corner gas station.

Most coin companies will mail their catalogues to you for a nominal price or sometimes for nothing. It is, then, a simple matter to check the coins you have against the coins in the catalogue.

If you should have a coin which you feel is of value, after checking it against a catalogue, do not send it to a dealer. Coins get lost in the mail and it is impossible to insure a coin properly unless you are certain of its value. Also, if the coin is not of value, time and mailing costs have been lost both on your part and on the part of the dealer.

It is far better to make a rubbing of the coin by placing it under a sheet of paper and rubbing gently across it with the edge of a pencil. Do this to both sides of the coin, and then forward the sheet of paper, *not* the coin, to the dealer. If he is interested and it is a rare coin, chances are good that he will reply by return mail.

Also, there are coin clubs in almost every area of the United States, and each member is interested in your coins. If they cannot afford to buy, they at least may tell you who can.

Any coin is worth checking—because it might be worth a fortune. What a shame it would be to spend a $100 nickel on five cent's worth of bubblegum.

An Imperial Easter Egg by Fabergé, about 1903. This magnificent piece is just one of the many priceless objects by the great St. Petersburg jeweler, some of which are missing.

The Metropolitan Museum of Art, Property of a private collector

Courtesy of Mr. Arpad D'Zurko

Mr. Arpad D'Zurko holds the violin which he bought as just another old instrument in a San Francisco shop. Today this violin has been authenticated as a genuine Stradivarius.

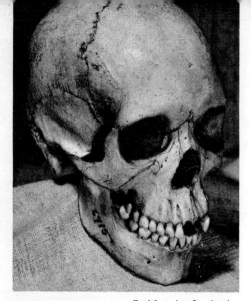

A skull of a member of the Kikuyu tribe, East Africa. A Wahehe skull, if it could be found, would be very similar to the one shown above.

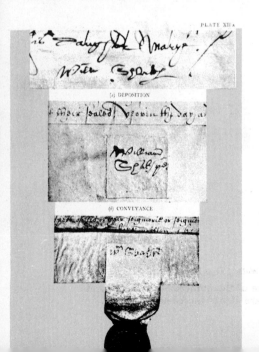

Three signatures of William Shakespeare. Estimates have been made that any new Shakespeare autograph found would be worth around one million dollars.

The Metropolitan Museum of Art

The "Chalice of Antioch," famous example of early Christian metalwork, 4th or 5th century. The Holy Grail might look very similar.

Musee du Louvre

An angel from Leonardo da Vinci's "Madonna of the Rocks." According to legend, Cecilia Gallerani was the model. Another painting of her by da Vinci is said to be missing.

REWARD!

WELLS, FARGO & CO.'S EXPRESS BOX, CON-
taining $160 in Gold Notes, was robbed this morning, by one man, on the route from Sonora
to Milton, near top of the Hill, between the river and Copperopolis.

$250

And one-fourth of any money recovered, will be paid
for arrest and conviction of the robber.

JOHN J. VALENTINE,

San Francisco, July 20, 1875.   General Sup't.

Wells Fargo Bank History Room

A Wells Fargo reward poster, one of the numerous items of memorabilia of the Old West that are being increasingly sought by collectors.

This is the famous 1804 silver dollar which has been sold at auction in excess of $28,000. Coins are constantly turning up for which collectors pay hundreds and thousands of times face value.

The Seamen's Bank for Savings

Two children's banks. Left, "Mammy and Child"; right, "Uncle Sam." These and other old mechanical banks are becoming increasingly collectors' items. Their value depends on design, age, and working condition.

A beautiful silver goblet by Paul Revere, 1782. Works by this famous American silversmith are today eagerly sought by collectors.

Museum of Fine Arts, Boston

Whaling Museum, New Bedford, Mass.

A Russell-Purrington panorama, one of the giant paintings which were popular in America some years ago. One of these panoramas, "Scenes of the Mississippi," by Banvard, is missing. It is said to be the largest painting in the world.

The Cullinan diamond in its rough state. Half of it weighed approximately 1⅓ pounds! The other half is missing, one of the great lost treasures of the world.

Campaign pins and buttons of yesterday are of great interest to to-day's collectors. Left, Lincoln For President button; right, Salmon P. Chase, later Chief Justice of Supreme Court, campaigned for presidential nomination in 1864.

XX

THE GOLDEN HORSESHOES

Lost Treasures of the Crusaders

THE legend of the golden horseshoes tells the story of a prince so magnificent that, when his horse lost its golden shoes on the road, the prince would not allow his men to pick them up.

The legend says that the name of the prince was Robert. It is possible that this was Robert the Magnificent, Duke of Normandy and son of William the Conqueror. But perhaps it was not he, since we know that Robert was obliged to pledge his dukedom to the King in order to raise money for a pilgrimage.

It is not terribly important to us today to know whether the personage of the legend was Robert, Duke of Normandy, or some other prince. What is important is the fact that both gems and pieces of gold were scattered along the road to Constantinople at some time, by some person or persons during the Middle Ages.

At this time there was a devotion to all things Christian; it was a day when all men dreamed of making a pilgrimage, and some men went on the long hard trek to all the sacred spots of Christendom. Some men sold their possessions or begged their way. They borrowed their boat passage or worked as best they could. And some men went with pageantry and riches and jewels. Such a man was he who shod his horses with shoes made of gold, shoes hammered in place with golden nails!

Some said that he was a prince from the land to the north of Rome. Others only stared in amazement as they saw him pass. He was followed on this pilgrimage by the men of his court, men arrayed in such magnificence that people gathered in awe-struck crowds to watch them pass.

As they rode and marched along the long road of the pilgrimage, the prince and his men would fling handfuls of money and jewels to the crowds. Pieces of gold were thrown onto the sides of the road for the mobs who scrambled in the dust for the precious pieces they were able to wrest from their neighbors. Pearls were cast down with the same gracious abandon by the prince and his men alike, until the roads were jammed with the poor, who waited impatiently for the noble pilgrims to let fall another priceless gem.

When they entered Rome in full splendor, and questions were asked, the people said that these men were princes of the north. The Pope himself gave the prince and his men a personal blessing before they took the road to Constantinople.

They traversed the road in splendor. The prince's horse had golden shoes hammered on with golden nails, it is true, but even golden shoes may be lost. On a long and rough journey such as the prince took, the horseshoe nails loosened and fell out one by one, until finally the shoes came off.

Has there ever been such a prince as this? Any other man would have had a servant reclaim the golden shoes. But this prince bade his servants leave them there in the dirt, so that no man could say that either he or his men would condescend to pick up such lowly things as horseshoes, even though the horseshoes were made of gold.

Perhaps a member of the crowd picked up the shoes and the golden nails. Perhaps not! It is possible that even today there rests, lodged in centuries of dirt, somewhere on the long road to Constantinople the golden horseshoes and golden nails of the prince we think may have been Robert the Magnificent, the fabulous Robert!

Even if you did not find the golden horseshoes and golden nails from the journey of Prince Robert, you could perhaps still find something of value from this period. Even if you could not find any pearls or pieces of gold that were cast into the dirt, you could still find items worth a great deal.

The swords the men carried, their horses' trappings, or even a record of the journey written by one of the men who followed Robert or any pilgrimage or any of the Crusades, would have value. For this was the age when men's eyes were first opened to the wonders of other lands. This was the age of the Crusades when men fought the Holy Wars. It was a time when men went out to fight and brought back with them spices and gems and silks, and, most important of all, knowledge.

It is almost impossible for us to believe today but in the Middle Ages, in the days of the pilgrimages and the Crusades, our civilization was in many respects not equal to the civilization of the infidel whom we had gone out to fight.

From meeting those other nations we learned a new kind of art, a new kind of architecture and design, new ideas in philosophy and techniques in mathematics. The Crusades themselves actually weakened the structures of European political life and gave a new impetus to an old thought about mankind—that all men were brothers.

In a sense, the treasure and the rewards left behind by the pilgrims and the Crusaders of the Middle Ages may have been, by this time, collected in full measure. To a degree, we owe to them everything we have: our art, our architecture, even the discovery of our nation.

XXI

PAGES AND PAGES OF GOLD

Rare and Valuable Editions

THE Codex Sinaiaticus, a portion of an ancient manuscript, was bought by the British Museum recently for a half a million dollars.

I have seen a market price of twenty-five thousand dollars quoted for Poe's *Murders in the Rue Morgue.* The first manuscript of *Alice in Wonderland* sold for almost seventy-five thousand dollars. A rare edition of Mark Twain's *Adventures of Tom Sawyer* sold recently for six hundred dollars. One edition of Shakespeare's works is worth as much as fifty thousand dollars—and it is still possible to find Shakespeareana, at least in book form.

In Sweden, a man found a small book in his home. It was only a small volume, but it was quite old and had obviously been brought to Sweden by the man's great grandfather when he had arrived there from England many years before. Realizing that the book might have value, the gentleman took it to the library of the University of Lund, Sweden, to have it evaluated.

News items about the little book appeared in print. In America, H. C. Folger read the story and within three hours he had an agent on the way to Sweden. Today, that little book, a first edition of *Titus Andronicus,* dated 1594, is a prized possession of the Folger Shakespeare Library in Washington, D.C.

There have, however, never been any such finds in America. Giles E. Dawson, curator of Books and Manuscripts at the Folger Shakespeare Library in Washington, states that he has never heard of any Shakespeareana having been found in America. There is, of course, always the possibility that someone might find a piece of Shakespeareana here which is both rare and valuable.

What may have been brought to America by immigrants is unknown. There might, today, in any of America's attics, be another piece of Shakespeareana, brought here as *Titus Andronicus* was taken to Sweden. And in whatever form they were, either written or printed, they would be valuable.

The original manuscripts of Shakespeare's plays are probably dust, but if not and if they could be found, they would be a treasure hunter's dream come true. Whereas many of the original manuscripts may have been destroyed by the printers, still others were used as wrapping paper by the grocers, since in those days it was the custom for grocers to buy manuscript pages for this purpose.

But suppose somewhere, somehow, the original manuscript of *Hamlet* has survived whole and undamaged? What is it worth? A million? Two million? Find it and see! Also, some of Shakespeare's plays that were separately put into quartos would be real finds. These were thought to be entirely worthless originally and were not even bound. As a result, they did not last long. They were destroyed through the ravages of wear and time.

It is of course possible that some of these might be hidden away somewhere in America's attics. Remember however that Shakespeareana must be *old* and *rare* to be valuable. The known values of Shakespeareana are as follows:

> **First folio edition** of his works, 1623 . . . as much as fifty thousand dollars
> **Second folio,** 1632 . . . less than two thousand dollars
> **Third folio,** many copies of which were destroyed in the Great Fire of London . . . today valued at close to thirty thousand dollars
> **Fourth folio,** 1685 . . . several hundred dollars
> **Nineteenth-century editions** . . . from one dollar to thirty dollars
> **The original manuscripts,** of course, would be of great value

Remember the wonderful Oz stories? One copy of *The Wonderful Wizard of Oz* sold for eight hundred and seventy-five dollars, although this is a very high price for this book. Three hundred and fifty dollars is far nearer the correct price. The eight-hundred-and-seventy-five-dollar copy was valued so high because the buyer wanted this particular copy very bady, not only because it was in such exceptionally fine condition, but because of the previous ownership of the book as well as the fact that *The Wonderful Wizard of Oz* is the rarest of Baum's books.

Today, rare editions of most of the Oz books are items for which the collectors will pay gladly. You might check your bookshelves for some of the following Oz books:

> **The Wonderful Wizard of Oz.** L. Frank Baum. Illustrated by W. W. Denslow (Chicago: George M. Hill, 1900). First issue: page 14, 1st line should read "low wail on the wind" instead of "low wail of the wind." Colophon printed on the back cover should be in eleven lines enclosed in a border. Worth about three hundred and fifty dollars.
> **The Marvelous Land of Oz.** L. Frank Baum. Illustrated by John R. Neill (Chicago: Reilly and Briton, 1904). First issue: copyright notice on back of title page lacks the line "Published, July, 1904." Worth about forty-five dollars.
> **A New Wonderland.** L. Frank Baum. Illustrated in color by Frank Verbeck (New York: R. H. Russell, 1900). Issued originally in pictorial boards and later in cloth. Worth about thirty-five dollars.

HORATIO Alger is another name to remember. Mr. Ralph Gardner, of New York, one of America's foremost collectors of the works of Horatio Alger, says that there are plenty of Algers still around in barns, cellars and attics. This is good news for the treasure hunter, since an Alger first edition can be worth anything from five dollars to one thousand dollars.

Horatio Alger was an American writer of juvenile books. During the 1800's, he wrote more than fifty books. There was a whole generation of Americans who delighted in these Alger stories which told, over and over, how any honest, hard-working American boy could go from rags to riches. The Alger boys became the heroes of any younger boy who wanted to get ahead in life.

One point to keep in mind, however, when searching for Alger books, is the fact that Alger also wrote under the pen names of Putnam and Hamilton. The titles listed below are only *some* of the Alger titles the collectors want, yet they are the rarest and most difficult to find.

Timothy Crump's Ward. Loring . . . one thousand dollars
Seeking His Fortune. Loring . . . five hundred dollars
Dan the Detective. Carleton . . . seventy-five dollars
The Western Boy. Any edition . . . seventy-five dollars
Tom the Bootblack. Oglivie . . . fifty dollars
Ralph Raymond's Heir (Hamilton). Gleason . . . fifty dollars
Paul the Peddler. Loring . . . twenty-five dollars
Young Outlaw. Loring . . . twenty-five dollars
Wren Winter's Triumph. Thompson and Thomas . . . fifteen dollars
Luke Walton. Porter and Coates (dark brown covers) . . . ten dollars

Old Alger paperbacks are also desired, and each of the following is worth about twenty-five dollars:

BURT'S BOYS' HOME LIBRARY:
Joe's Luck — #1
Tom Thatcher's Fortune — #11
Errand Boy — #14

MUNSEY'S POPULAR SERIES FOR BOYS AND GIRLS:
[Number 91] — #5
Tom Tracy — #10 (Putnam)

OGLIVIE, SUNSET SERIES:
Silas Snobden's Office Boy

BRAVE AND BOLD:
Ben Barclay's Courage — #105

STREET AND SMITH, MEDAL LIBRARY:
Adrift in New York — #243
Robert Coverdale's Struggle — #555

U. S. BOOK CO., LEATHER-CLAD TALES:
$500 — #23
Ned Newton — #24 (Putnam)
Mark Stanton — #25 (Putnam)
Erie Train Boy — #26
New York Boy — #30 (Putnam)
Dean Dunham — #32

Mr. Gardner will be happy to send out free lists of wanted Horatio Alger books to anyone who will send him a postage stamp for mailing costs. Address Mr. Ralph D. Gardner, 135 Central Park West, New York, New York.

Everyone knows the Edgar Rice Burroughs books, but not everyone knows that some of the editions of his books are worth from twenty dollars on up. The scarcest of his books are:

Age. First edition
Back to Stone. First edition
Lad and Lion. First edition
The Man Without a Soul. First edition
Tarzan of the Apes. First edition (McClurg)

The works of modern writers are often desired. For example, the first work by Hemingway would be worth around two hundred and fifty dollars.

Also, Elizabethan manuscripts are always collectors' items. Even as far back as the 1700's, the collectors realized this and accumulated them whenever and wherever possible. One gentleman of this period managed to obtain around fifty of these manuscripts. He made the mistake, however, of keeping them in the kitchen. Later, when he wanted them, he discovered that his servant had been under the impression that they had been left there as fire starters.

Very old miniature books in fine condition are collected by many people. And among the old Bibles which should be watched for are the Aiken Bible and the first edition of the King James Bible.

Original manuscripts of authors are always in demand, especially if the author is well known. Even the manuscripts of modern authors can be valuable. Not too long ago, the original manuscript of Tennessee Williams' *The Glass Menagerie* sold for six thousand dollars.

Older books are, many times, bound with pieces of other books on the insides of the bindings. If the book you find has a loose binding anywhere, it might be a good idea to see whether or not there is a piece of a printed page on the inside. Some very valuable fragments have been found this way.

Do not, however, rip away pieces of binding yourself to see whether or not there are fragments of printed matter inside. This would cause immense damage to a book or a binding that might have a great deal of value in itself. Instead, have the book checked first by an expert, or go through the lists of rare books that you can find in any library. If the book itself proves to be valueless, then you can start lifting away a small portion of the binding to see what is inside.

At the Folger Shakespeare Library in Wasington, D.C., old books are repaired whenever necessary, and one gentleman there is constantly on the watch for a fragment of *Hamlet,* even a piece of which in Shakespeare's handwriting would be priceless. At the Library, they have found several fragments from within the bindings which were valuable, but the gentleman is still looking for a piece of *Hamlet.*

Sometimes, old maps are found in old books, and these usually have some value. Letters written by famous authors can be valuable. A two-page letter from Charles Dickens can be worth a couple of hundred dollars, and a Longfellow letter has been sold for a little over a hundred dollars. The value of such letters would, of course, depend on their content as well as condition and demand.

There is a market for almost every kind of printed matter, and some people even collect old comic books—like Buck Rogers, Flash Gordon and Tarzan.

Old newspapers can have value. An auto dealer from Michigan found a copy of a newspaper dated April 23, 1849, in a car which he had taken in trade. When the newspaper was finally put up for auction, it brought seventy dollars. Remember, however, that old newspapers are not always worth this much—as always it depends upon supply and demand.

The so-called Penny Dreadfuls were cheap pamphlets dealing with the more spectacular aspects of crime. They were written for the public on the most blood-curdling killings of the latter part of the 1800's. Today these are collectors' items.

From 1732 to 1757, an almanac published by the author, Richard Saunders, was sold in the American colonies. Around ten thousand copies a year were printed. This means that there were approximately two hundred and fifty thousand copies of this almanac distributed to the public.

Today these copies are highly prized examples of Americana and, certainly, some of these two hundred and fifty thousand copies are still to be found in someone's attic or in second-hand stores.

Many people seeing a copy of this almanac might not recognize it at first, however, until they remember that Richard Saunders was Benjamin Franklin's pen name!

The Davy Crockett and the Commodore Rollingpin almanacs are also considered marketable. William Pierce, Cambridge, Mass., published the very first American almanac in 1639. As far as is known, no copy of this very first American almanac has ever been found.

MANY people will value the antique furniture their grandmother left them, the silver their aunt gave to them or the old gun that has been in the family for years, yet these very people will sometimes take a fortune in books out to the city dump and leave it there to be burned.

Sometimes, of course, the destruction of books is deliberate, as in the year 1797 when Napoleon Bonaparte destroyed the Golden Book of Venice. In this book the records and rolls of the city notables were written in letters of gold.

This would have been a valuable contribution to the collection of the bibliophiles if it had been left intact. Its value in terms of dollars and cents, however, is debatable, just as the value given for any rare book is debatable.

No matter what prices for rare books are quoted in this book or in any book, annual, catalog, etc., said prices must always be accepted for what they are: estimates only.

The price of rare books fluctuates from season to season, depending upon demand. Also, the condition of a book is very important. A book in really fine condition may sometimes sell for hundreds of dollars while the same book in poor condition may not be worth anything at all.

It is fairly safe however to watch for *old* and *rare* editions by the following authors:

> Elizabeth Browning
> Robert Browning
> Robert Burns
> Edgar Rice Burroughs
> Charles Dickens
> Charles L. Dodgson (Lewis Carroll)
> Charles and Mary Lamb
> Thomas Paine
> Mark Twain
> Jules Verne

Old and *rare* books on the following subjects are desired. But remember that only certain editions and authors are wanted.

> airplanes
> alchemy
> Americana
> art, drawing instructions
> atlases
> automobiles
> balloons
> bicycles
> blacksmithing

Bonaparte, Napoleon
buggies
cattle trade
cavalry
circusiana
Civil War
clocks
coins
crimes, murders, trials
Custer, General
directories, western, town, city, miners'
dolls
exploration
fire engines
guide books
guns
histories, town, city, county, state
horses
Indians
James, Jesse
Lincoln, Abraham
magic
Mayflower, passengers, voyage
medical books
military manuals
mines, lost
missions, California
Old West
outlaws
penny banks
pioneer life
pirates
plays
poetry
railroads
Revolution, American
school books
science
Southwest, early days of the
sports
theatrical items, actors, actresses
toys
travel
treasure, lost
Yellowstone National Park

Certain old issues of magazines are collectors' items also. A complete file of *Adventure* magazine has had, in the past, a market value of seven hundred and fifty dollars. Most old magazines, however, are not worth much, but if you should happen to have them in quantity, it would certainly be worth the time to try to sell them.

Also, a few copies may be worth from twenty-five dollars to one hundred dollars. Which copies they would be could only be decided by the collector. The wisest thing, of course, would be to show a collector or antique dealer what you have and let him decide which are the valuable ones.

The following list of magazines does not necessarily indicate that each copy of the magazines mentioned is valuable. Some of them may may turn out to be only worth a quarter. But some of the copies *might* be valuable. It is for the collector to say which ones are which.

> **Army Navy Weekly**
> **Argosy**
> **Black Mask**
> **Cosmopolitan**
> **Godey's**
> **Golden Argosy**
> **National Geographic**
> **New York Weekly**
> **Outdoor Life**
> **Peterson's**
> **Red Book**
> **Town and Country**
> **Vanity Fair**
> **Vogue**

Watch for the following kinds of catalogs:

> automobiles
> glass
> motorcycles
> musical instruments
> records
> silverware
> toys
> wagons

This does not mean that any book, magazine or catalog on the above subjects or by the above authors, etc., will have value. It means that the copy you have *might* be the one the dealers are looking for. The only way to find out for certain is to either check with your librarian or your neighborhood dealer.

XXII

PRINTS EXTRAORDINAIRE

Old Prints and Photographs

SOME time ago, an attorney ordered the destruction of thousands of lithographic prints. They were therefore taken to the city dump and burned.

The purpose of this destruction was to get rid of a quantity of items that were supposedly junk, in order to save space during the settling of the estate of a deceased lithographer. Those prints, if they could have been saved, would have been worth hundreds, possibly thousands of dollars to today's collectors, since the prints were Currier and Ives—and the deceased gentleman had been Nathaniel Currier himself.

One of those prints so wantonly destroyed by the flames might very well have been "The Life of a Hunter—A Tight Fix," identical with one that sold for three thousand dollars not too long ago.

In 1907, thousands of Currier and Ives prints were sold at auction. These prints, which were disposed of at that time for practically nothing, would be worth a small fortune if they could be gathered together again today. Today, Currier and Ives prints may be worth only a few dollars apiece or they may be worth thousands, depending as always on condition, rarity and demand.

A print that is one of a kind would naturally be worth a great deal more than one that is only one of many similar prints. And every so often a new print does turn up: a Currier and Ives print of which there was no known copy was found recently.

It would help in the search, of course, if one had an accurate list of all Currier and Ives prints that were made, but the firm of Currier and Ives did not leave a complete record of all their prints. For this reason, it is entirely possible for a person to locate a print so new that the collectors have never even heard of it.

Currier and Ives did issue catalogs, however, that list many of their prints, and some of the prints listed in these catalogs have never been found. They are, in the field of Currier and Ives prints, lost treasure.

It is entirely possible that hundreds of Currier and Ives prints are still stored away in America's attics waiting to be found. The list of subjects for Currier and Ives prints is almost endless—scenes of sports, the countryside, the city, battles, disasters, trains, ships at sea; winter scenes: anything was a proper subject for Currier and Ives.

Battle prints by Currier and Ives may sell for an average of twenty to thirty or forty dollars, although rare ones can sell for much more than this.

There were also prints made of the various Presidents. For example, a Currier and Ives print of John Adams sold recently for forty dollars. The Washingtons, both George and Martha, were subjects for Currier and Ives prints. One of these prints shows the death of Washington and portrays the President, his family, his servants and his doctor. Also portrayed on a Currier and Ives print was the body of President Lincoln as he lay in state.

Some of the most famous of the Currier and Ives prints are those referred to by the collectors as Darktowns. These were prints showing darktown comics, roller-skating scenes, darktown fire brigades, etc.

With so many prints having been made, the chances of finding another one, or even a new one, are good. Also, if you should find a print which looks as though it were meant to be colored by school children, don't throw it away, thinking it worthless. Currier and Ives did make prints especially for this purpose. They were printed uncolored, and then the colors were filled in by children.

The fact that a Currier and Ives print must be an original to be worth the attention of the collector is important. There were often hundreds of reproductions of each print made; but, to be a collectors' item, a print must be an original Currier and Ives.

Anyone who has heard of these famous prints and who finds a print he believes to be by Currier and Ives would doubtless have that print checked for authenticity and value—but it is quite possible that the same person might never have heard of Kurz and Allison prints and so might discard one if he found it. Yet Kurz and Allison prints are very much in demand. Prints such as the Kurz and Allison prints of Civil War generals always find a ready market.

Kellogg prints are also worth watching for. One Kellogg print, "The Boston Boys and General Gage," was recently put up for sale for sixty dollars. Prints of army officers and statesmen by printmakers Ehrgott, Forbriger and Co., are also in demand.

Old prints are probably among the easiest items to find—and the easiest items to overlook as having possible value. It is likely that in America, there are hundreds of prints stacked away in basements, attics and old trunks, waiting to be either destroyed or traded for cold cash depending entirely on the know-how of the finder.

Prints can be found anywhere! Sometimes they are stuck in picture frames behind old pictures; sometimes one may fall from the pages of an old book; sometimes you may find them in the linings of old trunks. They could be anywhere!

These prints may not be great works of art such as a Da Vinci, a Rembrandt or a Van Gogh, but still they are colorful representations of American life as it was known many years ago.

As times passes, historians must turn more and more to such items as these prints to learn how the common man lived. The history books may well record what actions were taken by which Presidents, but the old prints will tell us what kind of shoes they wore.

D O you have any old, unique and rare photographs relating to the history of photography? If so, there is a market for them. The George Eastman House in Rochester, New York, has a complete collection of various items relating to the history of photography—but they want more. They are especially desirous of obtaining personal documentation with regard to the famous personalities in the field of photography.

If you can find letters, diaries, notes on the field of photography by the following people, they want them:

> Daguerre
> Eastman
> Ives
> Mees
> Niepce
> Talbot

Remember that personal papers on photography do not necessarily relate to the above names, since there were many unknown and unsung experimenters in this field—and many of them will remain unknown until someone finds the documented evidence to prove they worked in the field at all.

Eastman House wants any items, if you can find them! As a matter of fact, they want almost anything that relates to cameras or photography. They want:

> autograph letters of the pioneers in the field
> books relating to the photographic field or the
>   men who worked in it
> cameras
> color transparencies
> daguerreotypes
> glass plates
> motion picture films
> notebooks and personal papers of the pioneers in the field

Eastman House, with the wonderful exhibits it already has, is well known in America. In one year alone, over two hundred thousand visitors came to view the exhibits at Eastman House.

Besides the items you would expect to see, there are also many of Eastman's personal possessions which are still in the house and are on view to the general public. The House, also called the George Eastman House of Photography, was originally Eastman's home, and not too many years ago, the home in which Eastman was born in Waterville, N.Y., was dismantled, shipped and put back together on the grounds of the Eastman House which is technically called the House of Photography.

Almost any antique dealer will buy old photographs. As a matter of fact, old photo albums of the Victorian era are collectors' items—with or without the photos inside. Even the empty albums have value. Photos from these old albums are collectors' items in themselves, their worth depending of course on who the subjects for the pictures were. If you have an old album, go through it to see if you recognize any of the figures there. There could be anyone represented, from Abraham Lincoln to Teddy Roosevelt.

The album might contain photos of Civil War soldiers, and there are collectors for them. Or the album might have photos of certain towns or cities. Chambers of Commerce or the town historical societies or libraries might want these. Photographs of doctors' offices, dental offices, stores, main streets, are all of value.

Or you might find pictures of complete families—great-grandparents, grandparents, etc., complete with all the nieces and cousins. Don't despair if you have never heard of these people. They don't have to be well known because, well known or not, the historical societies of a given area want them as they are a part of the history of that area. Genealogists also want these old albums that show the history of families. They are many times invaluable in filling in genealogical tables.

Think of the history we learn from these old photos. The things we deduce and think about and wonder about today are things we would have known for certain if the camera had been invented sooner. The whole panorama of history would have been laid before us if we had had photographs of the Middle Ages, the French Revolution or the Elizabethan period in England.

This loss of knowledge cannot happen again, because today we have records on film, as accurate as though they were still happening. We will no longer question history. We will look it up. Photographs are history as it happened—and for this reason, they are items worth collecting!

XXIII

GOLD DUST IN A BALL OF WAX

Carvings, Cigar-Store Indians,
Hitching Posts, Barbers' Poles

WHEN today's advertising man has a new idea, his confreres eye him skeptically and say, "All right, let's roll it up in a ball of wax and toss it around a little." When yesterday's store owner, who was also his own advertising man, had a new idea, his words on the subject were perhaps not as colorful but he would think it over a little and then hire a carver to make a figure that would be representative of his business.

After weeks of labor, the figure would be ready and would be proudly placed on display outside the door of the shop to let the passersby know the type of goods sold within. And if the figure was skillfully executed it would attract many viewers—and many buyers.

The purpose of advertising certainly has not changed, even though the gimmicks have. These older gimmicks, however, these carved figures of another day, are worth a great deal of money to the modern collector.

Perhaps, in our modern efforts to reach more people, we have neglected fine artistry. Perhaps this is one reason why collectors of today place such a high value on the advertising gimmicks of yesterday, for they are not only antiques but memories of a past which we will never see again.

All sorts of carved figures stood in front of the shops, and they were a familiar sight both in England and in America. Everyone who entered a shop passed one of these gaily painted figures as he went in.

Today their value is tremendous, depending, of course, upon condition, rarity, etc. A carved race track tout was recently appraised at over $2,000. Another shop figure, a captain, was appraised at over $3,000.

If you should find an odd figure, a real rarity, not just the run-of-the-mill cigar-store Indian, the chances are, if it is in good condition, that it is worth a great deal.

Yet even the cigar-store Indian can be worth at least something, depending again on age and condition. These wooden Indians were a symbol of the old-time American tobacco shops. They were a very common sight in the United States.

The cigar-store Indian industry in America was a going business selling approximately three hundred figures yearly, yet today there are only a few left, some of them in museums and collections. But perhaps there are many more around—waiting in your neighborhood lumber yard or even in your attic.

Sometimes these "Indians" are in bad condition, but, if you can find a collector who really wants one, it is possible that he would be willing to buy it first and then rejuvenate it.

In Westchester, California, there is a tobacco shop called Clyde's Pipe Rack, and in the front of the store stands Princess Minnehaha —a one-hundred-year-old wooden beauty, one of the last of America's wooden Indians. Not too long ago, however, Princess Minnehaha was in very sad condition, but the owners of the shop, Mr. and Mrs. Clyde Strawn, scraped away at the layers of old paint until they were down to the original—then carefully they repainted her to her original colors. Today Princess Minnehaha stands once more in front of a tobacco shop, as lovely as she was a hundred years ago.

Certainly if you could find a wooden Indian, it is worth investigating. The collectors are so avid that all members of the "Society for the Preservation of the Wooden Indian" have sworn to ". . . never . . . destroy their Indians and to let the Society know if they ever want to dispose of them, so they can be passed along to other collectors."

Any wooden Indian you may find is worth something, but there are other types of wooden figures, like the "Race Track Tout" and the "Ship Captain," which are worth a great deal of money. They are, however, more rare and harder to find and therefore of much greater value than the more common Indians.

Many of these figures which were not Indians were English, since the British "cigar-store Indians" were not Indians at all but "black boys" and "smoke shop figures."

One smoke shop figure, a sultan, was recently appraised at $525 —certainly worth watching for.

No one knows where all of these figures are today. They were eventually taken off the streets because of sidewalk restrictions. These ordinances killed one of our traditions, by causing the cigarstore Indian to pass into history—and on to the treasure hunter's list.

Not eliminated by these sidewalk restrictions, but fading from the scene simply because the march of progress made them obsolete, were the old-fashioned hitching posts.

They were put up by shop proprietors for their customers' convenience, in much the same way today's store owners provide parking lots for their customers.

Today the hitching post is forgotten—except by the collectors, who will pay as much as $250 for a rare and fine example.

There is one other item, however, which has not been eliminated from the American scene. Neither sidewalk restrictions nor modern progress has caused the barber pole to fade from our streets. But it is the *antique* barber pole which you should watch for; the modern ones, of course, are worth something only to the barbershop owner and not the collector.

The very old barber poles were complete with red pole, a bowl, and a strip of cloth. The red pole represented both the color of blood and the stick which the patient gripped tightly while the barber-surgeon did his job of blood-letting. The bowl would collect the dripping blood. The strip of cloth was used by the barber-surgeon to bandage his patient when he was through.

The barber's pole with the bowl was a rarity in America, but there were many of the more common bowl-less types which are now disappearing from the scene because people who do not realize that they are worth anything either destroy or throw them away.

Even a nineteenth-century barber's pole is worth around $60, and the older ones, of course, are worth much more. Whether you find a wooden shop figure or an old barber's pole, do not throw it away or burn it or repaint it. It may be something a collector would buy in a minute—if you would just give him a chance.

XXIV

Glass and More Glass

Venetian to Stiegel

THE world's most valuable example of the glass blower's art is the Portland Vase—a vase which the British Museum refused to sell even when offered fifty thousand dollars for it.

While it is extremely unlikely that the modern treasure hunter would find another Portland vase, still there are other examples of the glass blower's art which the treasure hunter should watch for.

Some of them will be worth only a few dollars, but some of them —if they finish out a set or if they are rare examples—can be worth a great deal.

Probably among the best known of the collectors' items—so rare and so valuable that most of the extant examples are in museums— are the glass objects of the Venetians. Venetian glass, as we know it, was made from the eleventh century until it reached its peak in the seventeenth century. There were, of course, other periods of Venetian glass making, but it is to these centuries that we must look for our museum pieces.

The art of glass making was so well regarded in Venice during this period that laws were passed regarding its manufacture. To protect the secrets of the methods which they used, the Venetians moved their entire glass industry onto the island of Murano, where armed guards walked the streets at night to protect the workers.

The workers themselves were executed if they betrayed the secrets of their profession, but if they were loyal to the industry they became prosperous.

Even exportation of the raw materials from which the glass was made was prohibited. Yet, even with all precautions, other nations sent in agents to try to learn the secret of how the fabled Venetian glass was made. It was not considered enough to merely have patrolling guards as protection against these foreign agents. Professional murderers were hired who eliminated the foreign agents, thereby "protecting" the secrets of the glass which today museums all over the world are anxious to have.

Among the most beautiful of the Venetian glass was the so-called "Cristallo" glass, which was very thin and which was twisted into many shapes. It was clear glass although it had a slight grayishness of color. There is also a type of Venetian glass that is white and clear combined and so finely woven that it is called "Lace Glass."

Yet, valuable as Venetian glass is, it is far more probable that the first thing the glass hunter will find will be American glass. Among these, if the treasure hunter is lucky enough, will be Wistar glass, Sandwich glass and Amelung glass.

Wistar glass is a "must" on the treasure hunter's list. In regard to the actual finding of Wistar glass, John C. Sheppard, Personnel Department, Glassboro Plant, Glassboro, N.J., says, "Whatever . . . (Wistar glass) . . . might be in existence would more than likely be in a museum." This does not, however, preclude the possibility that the treasure hunter might find a new and rare piece.

Caspar Wistar was a German button maker from Philadelphia. He imported glass workers from Belgium in the early 1700's and began his glassworks in a settlement called, appropriately enough, "Wistarberg," which was in the county which is now called Salem in New Jersey.

This Wistar factory was the first important glass factory in America. Window and bottle glass are among the important items to look for that were made in Caspar Wistar's factory. Other objects, such as bowls and household glass, were not made in the factory during working hours, but the workmen made these items for their own personal use to take home with them. They made them, supposedly, after working hours, and these, too, are items to watch for.

Caspar Wistar died in 1752. His son Richard carried on his father's business, until the year 1782. But there was another area where Wistar-type glass was made. The art was perpetuated as "Wistar type" glass by several workmen from Caspar Wistar's factory who also worked for themselves in Glassboro, N. J.

In 1781, according to local records, the Stanger Brothers, all four of them, went to Glassboro and opened a factory of their own. However, this factory failed and they sold it to Heston and Carpenter.

Heston and Carpenter sold out in their turn (shortly after 1800) to Ebenezer Whitney, and for over a hundred years the Whitney family made glass in Glassboro. Then they, too, sold out, this time to the Owens Bottle Company, which is still in operation today.

Thus, for over a hundred and fifteen years, Glassboro, New Jersey has produced glass which it is well for the treasure hunter to watch for, remembering of course that it will be the early pieces of this glass that you want.

Glass, either Wistar or "Wistar type" is well worth the time and effort of the vigilant treasure hunter.

Sandwich glass must also be on the treasure hunters' list. Worth from $10 or $15 apiece, every piece of Sandwich glass is worth something; and some pieces of Sandwich glass, if they are rare enough or finish out a collection, can fetch a great deal.

For example, a decanter of an ordinary Sandwich pattern sells for around $40 and a compote might sell for around $100—but find a piece of Sandwich that is rare or that can finish out a collector's set and you might get many times that amount.

Sandwich is a name familiar to all lovers of glassware and should be familiar to all treasure hunters as well, since collectors in all parts of the world desire rare and fine pieces of this glass.

Starting about 1825, glass was made in Sandwich, Massachusetts, and they continued to make it there for over fifty years by a process which has now been lost.

Until the 1820's glass was all hand blown, but at about this time Deming Jarvis, together with Enoch Robinson, made several machines which pressed glass by a process which made it possible to press glass into an iron mold and then stamp a pattern on it.

The new machines were so successful that old-fashioned glassmakers who were still trying to make a livelihood by hand-blowing glass became enraged at Deming Jarvis, because by using his machines, pressed glass could be produced at only a fraction of the cost of hand-blown glass.

Afraid that they would kill him, Jarvis hid. Yet, even though he had to hide in fear of his life, Jarvis continued working with his new machines. He was the owner of the Sandwich Glass Company, which became very successful.

Jarvis was ahead of his time in many ways. He was vitally interested in the welfare of his workmen, and he helped them to such an extent that they returned his help by enabling the Sandwich Glass Company to withstand even the depressions of the period.

Although pressed glass was made in many places, it was in Sandwich, Mass., that it found its niche in the world of fine glass—and found its way onto the treasure hunter's list.

The third well known type of American glass desired by collectors is Amelung glass, made in the Amelung Glass Factory, which was established near Frederick, Maryland, in the late 1700's. The factory failed, but the examples of their work—if you can find any of them—will be well worth your time. Some of these pieces of glass made in the Amelung factory were probably the only pieces of early American glass which were inscribed and dated.

There are many types of glass worth watching for. The list is almost endless. Patterned glass of any kind can be valuable. Certain pieces, of course, are very rare and therefore more sought after, like the "Bellflower" patterned cake plates which can be worth $250 apiece. Or the "Horn of Plenty" patterned dishes and cake plates which bring as much as $300 if they are of rare size and shape.

"Thumbprint" patterned punch bowls and compotes, in certain sizes, may be valued as high as $400; "Sandwich Star" patterned compotes can be worth $250; "Blackberry" patterned milk-white water pitchers are sometimes valued at a couple of hundred dollars.

All of them, of course, must be the ones that are the rare shapes, sizes, etc.

Also included among the American types to watch for is Amberina glass, a special type of glass into which gold had been put. The colors are amber, yellow and red, and the pieces were made during the nineteenth century in Massachusetts.

Peach Bloom glass, also made in Massachusetts during the same period, is another type to watch for. There are also examples of glass upon which are pressed scenes of historical interest, and these are of especial interest to American collectors. Examples of authentic milk glass are also highly prized—although there are so many reproductions of milk glass that what you do find will probably be merely another reproduction. Yet there is always the chance that you have found an authentic piece—and if you have, it belongs in the hands of the collectors.

There are also in America many types of European glass— shipped here as gifts, wedding presents, etc., or sometimes even for the commercial market—which are worth your time and effort. These would include the fabulous Bohemian glass of the 1500's; English crystal glass of the late 1600's; and the smoky blue glass of Waterford, Ireland, which was produced for over a century.

The list of types of glass to watch for is endless, and any piece of glass, if it is old enough, rare enough, and beautiful enough, should be investigated by the treasure hunter.

THE pastor of the little church steps down from the pulpit and hands one red rose—the year's annual rent—to the descendant of the Lord of the Manor. Feudal times? Europe in the Middle Ages? No! For the time is now and the place is a little town in Pennsylvania.

It is a strange thing to happen in our days, in our country, but it is so. It is the strange story which begins with two words: Glass— and Stiegel!

The words Stiegel and glass are synonymous with treasured glass —and the treasure hunter will do well to remember it. If he has what he thinks might be a piece of Stiegel ware I might suggest, as a reference, the book *Stiegel Glass* by William Hunter, with introduction and notes by Helen McKearin, 1950, New York, Dover Publications, Inc. This book may be used by the treasure hunter to familiarize himself with Stiegel ware as he searches for it, and to check what he has found against known items of Stiegel's.

One thing which the treasure hunter will soon discover is that there are certain colors which are of more value than other, more common, shades of Stiegel glass. Cobalt blue and amethyst are the two colors to especially look for, because these are the most unique.

Any example of Stiegel glass, however, is worth something to the treasure hunter. Stiegel glass of any kind is a rare find. There is, however, one pitfall open to the Stiegel hunter: there were many "Stiegel types" of glassware made both here and abroad.

But there are many authentic Stiegel items to watch for. He made many types and kinds of glass objects, from bottles, jugs, and salt cellars, to mustard pots, decanters and tumblers, and even window glass.

When searching for this glassware, it is also important to remember the age of the glass. The Stiegel glassworks were open from 1763 to 1774, making any glassware made in this factory very old by American standards.

Very old—and very fine—for Heinrich Wilhelm Stiegel did nothing halfway. In his factory he employed the very best of foreign workmen, and he also did something which was unheard of in that day. For his workmen he built a whole town—and for their education and happiness he built a church.

He called his little town Manheim. Today, Manheim, Pa., remembers Stiegel as one of its earliest and most illustrious citizens. The town remembers Stiegel as a man who lived in his own way—a way which harked back to feudal times. Manheim remembers Stiegel as the man who rode in fabulous coaches and lived like the old-time nobility. It remembers him as a man who loved riches and fine and expensive things.

He called himself Baron Stiegel. Today, no one knows for sure whether the title was authentic, but Stiegel certainly lived like a Baron.

It is known definitely that he was born in Germany and that he came to America as a very young man, arriving in Philadelphia in 1750. Very little else is known about him. We do know, however, that he became famous and wealthy, and that he loved his wealth, and that he spent money so lavishly that his extravagances eventually broke him.

He lost everything, and he died a forgotten man. Even his grave was not considered important enough to remember.

By the time the people of Manheim awoke to the fact that one of their most illustrious citizens had died—and that he should be remembered by them—it was too late, and his grave has not been located to this day.

Even though Manheim forgot Stiegel as he lay dying, Stiegel remembered Manheim. As one of his last acts he willed a parcel of ground he owned in Manheim to the congregation of the Zion Lutheran Church. This was the little church that Stiegel himself had named.

Today Manheim—belatedly—remembers Stiegel in a ceremony which is known as the "Feast of the Roses," held on the first Sunday of June every year. One red rose is handed, by the pastor of the church, to a descendant of the "Baron" Stiegel.

This red rose is the year's rent for the use of the lot which Stiegel willed to the church. This annual payment of a rose was stipulated in the will which Stiegel himself had made in that grand and feudal manner which he loved so well.

Yet even without his "Feast of the Roses" Stiegel would be remembered as long as collectors search for specimens of fine and treasured glass.

The treasure hunter will do well to remember him, too.

XXV

Miscellanea

Clothing, Clocks and Bells

WHEN the Queen of France was crowned, at the beginning of the seventeenth century, she wore a fantastically beautiful dress that glittered with diamonds. The dress itself was completely hidden beneath the brilliant display of gems. Even royalty has its troubles, however, and it became necessary to pawn the dress to one Marshal d'Ancre.

In 1616, as French political feelings swayed back and forth like the pendulum on a clock, mobs attacked D'Ancre's home. They looted, tore and ransacked the house, and, when it was over, the diamond-covered dress had been ripped apart, and only pieces of it were left. Whether any of these pieces survived, we do not know. It is at least a possibility, however, that some of them might still be able to be located.

But a dress does not have to be diamond-covered to be valuable. Incredible though it may sound, there is a collector of costumes who is looking desperately for a Dior "New Look." For some reason these dresses are hard to find. This New Look, of course, has to be of a particular period—and you must remember that Dior has had many New Looks.

Antique clothing of several hundred years ago is well worth digging out of your attic! Clothing from the Victorian era and of the

Twenties would have little monetary value, although in my opinion it would have enough value to be worth the effort of having it appraised. Easiest to find of these clothing items are wedding gowns and christening dresses, since these items would often have been packed away after they were once worn, whereas most everyday clothing would have been worn out through use. The hardest items to find, then, are the everyday garments of fifty or a hundred years ago—the afternoon dresses, the gingham dresses and the storied calico prints.

The young woman of the early 1900's often wore a sort of outfit called a Peter Thompson. It was a two-piece sailor outfit, complete with middy blouse and wide collar. These costumes are collectors' items today. Shawls are also collectors' items, and old hats are becoming harder and harder to find.

I am sure that an antique corset, say one from the Victorian era, might have some value, but it would have to be as famous as the one that belonged to Catherine de' Medici for it to be placed in the museum class. Catherine's corset, according to one authority, was made of metal and weighed approximately thirty-five pounds.

There are very few collectors of historical clothing in America, clothing, that is, of the Victorian era and the Twenties. Older brocades and silks, etc., are of course museum pieces and are in another class entirely.

Antique fabrics of all kinds are worth watching for. Mrs. William H. Reals, of Chicago, Ill., is one of America's foremost private collectors of antique fabrics. According to Mrs. Reals, available today in fair amounts for collectors are French eighteenth-century brocades, French printed cottons and American cottons showing our Presidential candidates.

Also according to Mrs. Reals, mummy cloths are collectors' items. Mummy cloth found in Egypt and Peru is the oldest cloth in the world, at least the oldest of which pieces of any size are in existence. Made of very finely woven linen, Egyptian mummy cloth has approximately five hundred threads to the inch. Today even good percale is nowhere near as fine. The closest thing we have today to the Egyptian cloth is very fine-quality silk. The process by which this cloth was woven is unknown.

From mummy cloths to old coverlets, almost any kind of old fabric has some value. Not too long ago, an eighteenth-century Spanish

Louis Quinze-style coverlet was sold for a high price at an auction. Antique American quilts and colonial coverlets are collectors' items. Nineteenth-century fabrics are worth checking, especially pieces of cotton with the manufacturer's name on them.

The following types of clothing and fabrics are especially desired:

> boots
> embroidered items
> knickers
> men's straw hats
> Victorian piano covers

A NURNBERG Egg is not an egg at all, but a watch. These were watches shaped rather like eggs and made in Nürnberg, Germany, in the early 1500's. Not only these, but watches of all kinds, sizes and shapes made in the past are now collectors' items.

Watches date back to the time of the Renaissance. Diamonds, various gems and enameled pictures decorate some of the most beautiful of the older watches. Remember that some of these older watches were very heavy, and also that the minute hand of the watch was not developed until the 1680's. Before this time, watches had no minute hands.

Some of the very old watches had built-in sun dials, because the watches themselves, even when in perfect condition, did not keep good time.

Back in the 1890's, there were watches with pictures inside them, made only for adult eyes—and today they are collectors' items, though still only for adult eyes. In their own way, these watches were works of art, with enamel bows in the lady's lingerie and diamonds in her garters. They were without a doubt pornographic. They were in a double case, and one had to know the secret of the watch in order to open the dust case and see the picture inside.

According to W. C. Harding, clock enthusiast, a list of American clocks that are scarce, that have some monetary value and that might still be found in America's attics, would include the following:

> **Banjo, lyre, and shelf clocks** by Simon Willard, Aaron Willard, Sr., and Aaron Willard, Jr.
> **Tall case or grandfather clocks** by the Willards
> **Shelf clocks** by Eli Terry
> **Shelf clocks** by Silas B. Terry, especially those having balance-wheel escapement and no pendulum

Shelf clocks by Joseph Ives, especially those deriving power from flat, leaf-type springs, as distinguished from flat rolled or coiled springs.
Clocks with the above type of power by Atkins and Fuller.

REMEMBER the bell whose peal was synonymous with the little red schoolhouse? Those bells are collectors' items today. Even cowbells are collectible.

The making of bells goes back hundreds of years. Bells come in all sizes, from very tiny to huge; and they were made in the shape of people and animals, as well as in the standard bell shape.

Over three hundred of the four hundred bells that originally lined the El Camino Real highway in California have disappeared. Each of them bears the dates 1769-1906, if you should happen to find one.

Bell collectors seem to go in for large collections, when they can. Lawrence Altman of St. Louis, Mo., for instance, one of our foremost bell collectors, has a collection of over seven hundred bells.

Watch for bells made of:

> brass
> glass
> iron
> marble
> pewter
> silver

Watch for the following kinds of bells:

> Chinese bells
> church bells
> curfew bells
> Early American bells
> fire bells
> horse bells
> unusual-looking bells

XXVI

FURNITURE

Chippendale to Franklin

THERE is a magic name in the world of furniture—so magic that even the furniture just made in the style for which he was famous is worth a fortune. His name is Thomas Chippendale.

He has been called the greatest of all the world's furniture makers. Today, if you can find anything in the "Chippendale" manner, if it is old enough and in fine enough condition, it can be worth a fortune.

A Chippendale desk can be worth as much as $36,000—or even more. Chippendale chairs can be worth $200 or $300 apiece, and some of them have been valued as high as $500 or $600 each.

Any Chippendale table is worth hundreds of dollars—and anything else that can be authenticated as Chippendale is worth a great deal.

One woman, at least according to one story, found this out by trying to sell some old "junk." She thought it was junk until the dealers saw it and labeled it "treasure." There was some old silver, dating back two centuries. And the furniture? Part of it was Sheraton—and part of it was Chippendale!

When they were through evaluating her old "junk" they paid her $100,000 for it!

While you are gasping at the great amount she received for her old Chippendale and silver, do not forget the name of Sheraton, for this is another name in furniture which carries with it both magic and dollars for the finder.

Sheraton was the eighteenth-century furniture designer who never even owned his own shop. He did not even make a good living for himself. He was a jack of all trades: preacher, teacher, writer—and furniture designer.

Today a Sheraton cabinet can be sold for around $500—if you can find it. Or one of his tables can be worth $1,000 or more, if it is in fine condition.

Perhaps that old piece of furniture which you found may be neither Chippendale nor Sheraton. It might be Hepplewhite! It might even be a Hepplewhite Secretaire bookcase worth $1,000.

Or it might be a piece of Adams furniture worth, certainly, a great deal. These pieces of lost furniture could be anywhere! When looking for lost treasures of this kind, there is no limit as to where they might be.

In your attic, your cellar, the second-hand store—or even in your yard, like the ten-thousand-pound, inlaid-marble, sixteenth-century table which was found in the yard of an English house wrecker.

Anywhere at all! And they could have traveled thousands of miles before they came to rest in your neighborhood second-hand store! The inlaid-marble table had originally been designed for a Roman palace—but the yard in which it was rediscovered belonged to a house wrecker!

The piece of furniture you find may have traveled all the way across the ocean to some family who liked European imported goods. Only to be lost again through war or misfortune—or by simply being thrown out by descendants of the original owners, because they did not know what they had.

What they threw out may even have been a Louis XV table worth thousands of dollars. Perhaps it may have been fine enough to have brought in a sale almost as much as one Louis XV table which was sold recently. This particular table was sold for $100,000!

So take another look at that old "junky table" in the attic. It could be Louis XV. Or it might be only a Provincial table, made contemporarily with, but in imitation of, the Louis XV style. Yet even if it is Provincial, it would still be worth hundreds of dollars.

Or it could be a Louis XV chair worth thousands of dollars—or it could be a chair of the later period, called Louis XVI and still be worth over $1,000. Or a Louis XVI table worth $5,000 or more.

From a later period, when Napoleon sat on the throne of France, you might find furniture of the Directoire and Empire periods, worth several hundred dollars apiece.

Or you might find items of the so-called Regency type, chairs worth hundreds of dollars apiece, or sofas of the same period, also worth hundreds of dollars each. Or a Regency stand worth $500 or more. Also watch for Queen Anne furniture, some of it worth many thousands of dollars.

Any piece of furniture, if it is old enough and rare enough, can be worth something. Like the miniatures which were so prevalent at one time. One story is that they were made for children. Another story is that they were made by apprentice furniture makers to show the quality of their work. But for whatever reason they were made, they are worth something today. A miniature chest of drawers, for example, is worth from $60 to $70.

Even such odd items of furniture as *papier mâché* tables and chairs are worth something. A *papier mâché* chair can be worth a couple of hundred dollars—and a *papier mâché* table can be worth even more.

Whatever it is, if it is of fine craftsmanship, is old enough, and has the proper lines, it is valuable.

It takes an expert, of course, to properly evaluate a piece of old furniture, but you can learn the different styles of furniture and therefore know what to look for. Your librarian can give you books with pictures of the various styles. Most encyclopedias have pictures showing examples of the different makes and styles of furniture. You can go to your local museums and see examples of fine furniture. Remembering what you have seen there, you will know what to look for the next time you go treasure hunting for lost furniture.

When you find a piece that looks old to you, look for wear on the corners and on the bottoms of the legs. Watch for old-fashioned nails or wooden pegs. And just plain beauty! For there is nothing quite so beautiful as an antique chair or table. Or if you are the kind who does not like antiques, then look again and imagine the hundreds or thousands of dollars which you can sell it for! And it will look just as beautiful to you as it will to the collector who will gladly dig deep in his pocket for cold, hard cash.

A DUNCAN PHYFE table can be worth almost $1,000—if you can find it!

So can any other piece of furniture labeled as connected with the Scotsman Phyfe, who came to America to become one of our most famous furniture designers. Watch for any piece of his furniture— for, if authenticated, it is worth a small fortune.

The value of a piece of furniture, however, is sometimes over-shadowed by the historical importance of it. Such as the furniture made by John Alden! Today, where are all of the pieces which he must have made for his Priscilla? Some of it, perhaps, in the museums, but some of it, perhaps, in your attic—if you would only take the time and trouble to look!

When John Alden died, he was an old man of eighty-eight, and surely during his lifetime he must have produced many items— which you might possibly find if you are lucky.

In looking for furniture by John Alden, however, do not overlook the furniture of the rest of the early settlers. Any furniture belonging to or made by any of the Pilgrims who came over on the Mayflower has value today.

Remember the Pilgrim names of Carver and Brewster, for furniture connected with their names has value. It has not been too many years since a Carver chair was sold for $1,000.

Or remember the chair made by another of our early Americans —the legendary rocking chair of Benjamin Franklin. The story goes that Franklin invented the rocking chair because he was uncomfortable in his old straight chair. He solved his problem by putting rockers on it.

The story is a legend, and it may or may not be true! Franklin's so-called rocking chair may have been confused, in the story, with his fan chair, which he did invent and which is missing.

Certainly we know that the fan chair existed, because at least one person saw it—and recorded what he saw. In 1787, the Reverend Dr. Manasseh Cutler, visiting Franklin, saw an article of furniture which he describes as "his (Franklin's) great armchair, with rockers, and a large fan placed over it, with which he fans himself, keeps off the flies, etc., while he sits reading, with only a small motion of the foot. . . ."

Every museum curator and every collector in America would grab at this chair—if you could find it.

Anything made in the early part of American history can have value, if old enough, fine enough, and rare enough. Chests have been known to bring from $500 to over $5,000. Cupboards can be worth several hundred dollars. Tables can be worth a couple of hundred dollars. Anything from this period is worth investigating.

Also, while investigating furniture from this period, do not forget the furniture of the later era named for Victoria of England. Pieces in this style are becoming rarer and more expensive by the day.

Already some of the finer examples have been valued at several hundred dollars apiece, and as the fad for Victoriana increases, so will the value of each piece.

So do not throw away your great-aunt's old chair or sofa which you have been hiding in the attic. Take it out and have another look at it.

Furniture which you think is junk might turn out to be fortune in disguise. You could have anything from an early Phyfe to the rocking chair of Benjamin Franklin.

XXVII

Diamonds All Around You

Where to Look for Them

A FARMER'S children kept finding pretty pebbles in the yard
—pebbles which they thought were pretty playthings. Their
mother gave one of them to a neighbor, who sold the pebble for
several pounds—and the word was out. Diamonds had been discovered in South Africa!

Many years later, in faraway Brazil, two farmers walked along
the path of a dry river bed. A stone glinted in the sunlight and they
passed it by. Later, his curiosity aroused, one of them returned.
The stone turned out to be the seven-hundred-and-twenty-six-and-
a-half-carat Vargas diamond.

Fabulous finds, but no one seems to think it so strange, because
the finds were made in other countries. Yet here in the United
States, diamonds have been found in the past—and will be again
if you know where to look for them.

In 1906 a farmer in Arkansas was doing his plowing—and uncovered a two-and-three-quarter-carat diamond. This was the beginning of the Arkansas diamond field.

Today our Arkansas field is limited in output—but while it was in
full operation more than fifty thousand diamonds were taken out,
the largest of them weighing forty carats. Today, however, you can
still find diamonds in Arkansas, because there is a place called the
"Crater of Diamonds" near Murfreesboro which is open to the public and where anyone can hunt for diamonds.

Only a few years ago a housewife on vacation went to the Crater of Diamonds and found a fifteen-and-one-half-carat diamond. It was named the "Star of Arkansas." A couple of years later a man and his wife found a three-carat diamond worth over two thousand dollars. And there are more diamonds in the Crater of Diamonds—waiting for you to find them. If they are less than five carats you get to keep them, but if they are over five you must give a percentage to the people who own the property. Still, this is treasure. Who would not be willing to share a percentage of a ten- or twelve-carat diamond—just for the right to look for it!

But there are other places right here in the United States where you can find diamonds. In 1928, in the town of Peterstown, West Virginia, a father and son set up a game of horseshoes in a vacant lot. It was a game of horseshoes which they will never forget—for during the course of that game they accidentally discovered the "Punch Jones," a thirty-four-carat diamond.

The West Virginia diamond is a little different from the Arkansas diamond. For this is a glacier diamond, swept downwards thousands of years ago by the onslaught of the glaciers, the big ice that swept everything before it—including diamonds.

There are many states wherein glacier diamonds have been found, but the point, of course, is that the glaciers swept them away from some particular place—a mother lode, probably somewhere in Canada.

This mother lode has never been found, and its extent is anyone's guess. Perhaps the big ice swept all the diamonds before it—or, again, we may have another Kimberley in our northern back yard. We never will know, until some treasure hunter finds it.

Another Kimberley sounds fantastic, yet by tracing the paths of the glaciers and by knowing that glacier diamonds have been found in those paths, we know that there is at least a possibility of a rich and fabulous mother lode somewhere in Canada, probably in the Hudson Bay region.

Glacier diamonds have been found in many states, particularly of course in the Great Lakes states, but even in West Virginia it is wise to watch for them. You might find another Punch Jones!

Glacier diamonds, however, are not the only diamonds to watch for. In California alone over two hundred diamonds have been "accidentally" found by men who were gold mining. They turned up during ordinary gold panning operations.

Diamonds have been found from one end of the United States to the other—in a country where most people might not even glance twice at the shiny pebble they saw while they were on their Sunday picnic or summer vacation. But remember the two Brazilian farmers who passed by the Vargas diamond. Only one of them was curious enough to go back and look it over again.

A diamond of gem quality can be worth $1,000 a carat, but the lesser-quality diamond, the industrial diamond, is so badly needed by industry that, if you could find them a good source of industrial diamonds, they would welcome you with open arms.

It takes the industrial diamond to successfully operate many modern production plants. Today, our need for the home production of industrial diamonds has become so acute that the United States Bureau of Mines has begun a project to prospect for them.

More romantic than industrial diamonds, of course, is the treasure hunter's hope of finding a magnificent, large, gem stone—but first he must be able to recognize one if he should find it. A diamond in the rough does not look like the lovely, sparkling gem that we see in a jeweler's window.

True, it is as hard; but it is not as pretty. It has a glassy or frosty appearance, and it sometimes feels greasy to the fingers as you rub it, and many times it looks just like certain types of quartz. Yet, while both quartz and diamond will scratch glass, the diamond will scratch the quartz.

Diamonds, to be gem stones, should be free of all blemishes or flaws. They are clear stones, yet a deeply colored stone may become a stone of great value—like the Blue Hope diamond.

When you are looking for diamonds, do not throw away frosted or glassy looking stones because of their odd color. Diamonds come in all colors. They can be yellow or green, blue or pink, brown or red, gray or black.

Any color—and almost anywhere. Watch for them in the dirt, imbedded in rocks, in sand, in the gravel of dried-up river beds, and in the rippling brooks. Diamonds have been found in many such California streams leading down from the Sierra Nevada. They have been found in the Great Lakes region, on the Pacific coast, and in the Atlantic-Piedmont region.

You can look for them almost anywhere. More specifically you can look for them in the following areas:

Alabama: Lee, Shelby Counties

Arkansas: Pike County: Murfreesboro

California: Amador County: Indian Gulch, Volcano
Butte County: Cherokee Flats, Oroville and Yankee Hill
Del Norte County: Smith River
Eldorado County: Placerville and Webber Hill
Nevada County: French Corral
Plumas County: Spanish Creek and Gopher Hill
Trinity County: Trinity River
Tulare County: Alpine Creek

Georgia: White County: Harshaw Mine, Acooche Valley
Clayton County: Morrow Station
Hall County: Gainesville

Idaho: Ada County: Diamond basin

Indiana: Morgan County: Martinsville
Brown County: Lick Creek near Morgantown

Kentucky: Russell County: Cabin Fork Creek

Michigan: Cass County: Dowagiac

Montana: Glacier County: Nelson Hill near Blackfoot

North Carolina: Burke County: Brindletown Creek Ford
Cleveland County: King's Mountain
Franklin County: Portis mine
Lincoln County: Cottage Home
McDowell County: Headwaters of Muddy Creek, Dysortville
Mecklenburg County: Todd Branch
Rutherford County: Twetty's mine

Ohio: Clermont County: Milford near Cincinnati

South Carolina: Spartanburg County

Tennessee: Roane County: Clinch River near Union Crossroads

Texas: Walker County: Huntsville

Virginia: Chesterfield County: Manchester

West Virgina: Monroe County: Petterstown

Wisconsin: Dane County: Oregon
Ozaukee County: Saukville
Pierce County: Plum creek
Racine County: Burlington
Washington County: Kohlsville
Waukesha County: Eagle

XXVIII

FOUR-ALARM TREASURE

Fire Marks of Yesteryear

DO you know that a fire mark can be worth a thousand dollars? Or do you even know what it is?

Have you ever looked at the side of an old building—and seen a plate or plaque nailed securely to the wall? Have you ever wondered what it was? Well, chances are good that it was a fire mark, telling firemen that this building was insured by the company whose name or emblem was illustrated on the plaque.

The fire mark was placed on the outside of a building so that the fire brigade—and anyone else interested—would know that the building was insured and by which company.

Fire marks were always placed on the *outside* of a building. They are usually to be found on an old building between the first and second floors rather than on the ground floor, because this prevented the fire mark from being destroyed or removed by pranksters or children.

However, in towns along the rivers, the treasure hunter must search as high as six stories up for the fire mark, which was placed so high because of the floods which are common in some river towns. Located well above the water line of the highest possible flood stage, the fire marks were in plain view at all times and the firemen could easily tell who insured the building.

Fire marks were first used in Europe, where they have been

known for almost three hundred years, but in both Europe and America each company adopted its own particular fire mark.

In Europe, in the early days of their history, the fire marks identified property insured by a particular company, so that the insurance companies, which had their own fire brigades, could put out fires on properties which were marked by their own particular fire mark.

American fire marks were first used in the 1750's although even before then America had organized methods of fire fighting. In 1696 bucket brigades were formed. In 1718 the first fire engine was brought over from London; and in 1721 we find a public chimney sweep appointed, although this was in the line of fire prevention rather than fire fighting.

In 1735 the first fire brigade was formed, and in 1752 the first American fire insurance company was formed. In America, the fire brigades knew that the insurance company, whose mark was on a building, would reward the fire brigade which successfully put out the fire. And if two or more brigades showed up to put out the fire, many times fights broke out among the firemen, with bloody noses and black eyes attesting to their claim that their brigade, and their brigade alone, was the one which put out the fire.

Many times the fights took place—with each brigade using their fists to prove that they got there first with the best men and the best equipment—while the fire raged on. Sometimes the building burned down before the fire fighters stopped fighting each other.

If the brigades arrived at a building which did not have a fire mark—they turned around and went home, and the building burned merrily down.

The use of the fire mark has died away until today it is an almost forgotten piece of early Americana—but not to the collector of fire marks, for to him the tradition lives on.

American fire marks have been made of tin, cast iron, and lead. Fire marks have also been made of brass, copper and zinc. And some comparatively recent fire marks were made of porcelain or enamel upon iron.

Probably one of the most interesting searches for lost treasures ever made was the search made for the first fire mark put out by the Insurance Company of North America. It was "A wavy star of six points, cast in lead and mounted on a wooden shield."

The first fire mark of this company—the star design—was issued in 1794, but later other designs replaced this one. But it was the "star" which every collector wanted.

In 1914, it was believed that no star designs were in existence. In 1915 it was believed that the star variety had been lost forever. In 1928 the star design was still believed to have been all destroyed.

Yet a year later, on an old building on Pace Street, near Second, in the city of Philadelphia, a collector noticed an unusual stain on the face of the building. Being a collector, he noticed immediately that the stain was the same size and shape as the shield which records said was the shield of the star design.

He located the owner of the building—and then the owner's father, and then the owner's grandfather. Finally, after many questions and searchings, the shield was found—in the hands of a carpenter.

Believing himself, happily, in possession of the lost "star," imagine the collector's disappointment when he discovered that while the shield was the right size and shape, the design nailed to it was another design entirely—one which was not rare at all.

But, not ready to give up, he carefully examined what he had and discovered, underneath the not-so-rare fire mark, an outline—the outline of a star.

Careful questioning brought out the facts that the star had been sold years before to a second-hand dealer from Baltimore. Then the search began in earnest. Every antique and second-hand store in Baltimore was searched and their managers and owners questioned with regard to the star.

Finally, on the outskirts of the city, the star was found. It had been gathering dust for years on the shelves of the shop. Even then, however, the collector was not satisfied. First he applied chemical tests to prove the age of the star. Then he tried the star against the shield—and it fitted, "nail hole for nail hole, line for line!"

Today, that star is with the collection of the Insurance Company of North America Companies, and it is exhibited at 1600 Arch street in Philadelphia, which now has not one star design but two.

C. A. Palmer, of that company, states almost sadly, ". . . this company's first mark, the six-pointed lead star on wood, is so rare . . . there being only two in existence that we know of, that from a monetary point of view, no amount of money would produce another one, and fortunately one of these rare marks was donated to us, whereas the other cost us $500."

The treasure hunter's challenge here is obvious—find another "star."

The value of fire marks, as in coin collecting, is based on rarity and condition. Rare marks are worth from $200 to $1,000 apiece, depending on age and condition. There are certain lone fire marks which are unique, however, and if a new, unique mark were to be discovered, it would be quite valuable.

Below are listed fire marks which are considered rare, worth on an average around $200 apiece.

> **Philadelphia Contributionship:** (1) Fancy or scalloped design shield— four interlocking hands, issued about 1765. (2) Shield has rounded top and bevel edge, issue of 1774. (3) Shield is plain edged board, issued about 1776. (4) Much smaller than above, issue of 1815, oddly shaped plaque. (5) Issue of 1819, small hands.

> **Mutual Assurance Company for Insuring Houses from Loss by Fire, Philadelphia:** (1) Design of the "Green Tree"—dated 1784— shows a leaden tree on a bevelled-edge shield of wood. (2) Absence of bevelled edge, issue of 1797. (3) First of the elliptical wooden shields, issued in 1799. (4) Issue of 1803, shield much smaller than the first oval—last wooden mark issued by the company. (5) The first all-iron mark of the "Green Tree" and largest of its iron varieties—this one measures thirteen inches from top to bottom. Known as the "large flat back," issue of 1805. (6) Issue of 1806—known as "small flat back"—the second iron mark issued by this company. (7) Not more than three dozen of this squatty iron variety are known to have been issued, dates from 1827.

> **Insurance Company of North America:** (1) Leaden eagle on a wooden plaque. The marks dated 1794 are the famous "star" fire marks but after December 26, 1796, the insured had a choice of this leaden eagle or the six-pointed star. (2) Copper eagle rising from a cloud. This mark has a rolled edge and came into use just after 1800. Not more than six specimens are known to exist. (3) Iron eagle, differing slightly from the copper eagle. This mark was first issued in 1830 and has a beaded edge.

> **Fire Association of Philadelphia:** (1) Fire Association mark dating 1817. Flat and made of iron, with a full stream of water gushing from a hose attached to an old-time fire plug. The letters "F.A." were gilded, as were the plug and hose. The grass at the base of the hydrant was green. (2) Also an extremely flat, iron variety, except that water is not gushing from the hose. This is the only mark made by the Fire Association with a short hose ending to

the right of the center of the mark; issue of 1825. (3) Made of lead; issued 1857. (4) Made of brass. Only twelve issued; some have many sets of numbers in gilt; dates about 1859. Rarest of all issues of this company.

Hope Mutual Insurance Company of Philadelphia: (1) Issued in 1854, an oval iron casting with beaded edge, showing in center a figure of "Hope" resting on an anchor.

United Firemen's Insurance Company of Philadelphia: (1) Issue of 1860; very large, heavy iron casting. Has three holes for attaching to houses, whereas later marks have the regulation two holes.

City Insurance Company of Cincinnati, Ohio: (1) This company went out of business before 1850; the fire mark was issued about 1846. It is a large, iron casting, showing an old-type fire engine with crew. The mark is distinctive by reason of its very fancy shape.

Union Insurance Company, Charleston, S.C.: (1) Founded on June 17, 1807, the company retired about 1839. The fire mark, an oval casting, tells the story of fire insurance. On one side, a building in flames, on the other, a new building. All Charleston fire marks are rare, as the town was partially destroyed by fire on many occasions between 1700 and 1900.

Mutual Insurance Company, Charleston, S.C.: (1) Issued about 1798; an oval, iron casting, the mark shows a guardian angel hovering over a city, sprinkling water on fire. First iron fire mark made in America.

United States Insurance Company of Baltimore, Md.: (1) Issued in 1834; oblong, almost square, iron casting.

Fire Insurance Company of New Orleans, La.: (1) This mark has, in both design and initials, a most striking resemblance to the mark of the Fire Association of Philadelphia. Oval, iron casting, issued in 1806, a year after the founding of the company.

Mobile Fire Department Insurance Company, Mobile, Ala.: (1) Company founded in 1866; retired in 1879. The mark is an iron casting showing a fireman's hat and company's initials in raised letters.

Baltimore Equitable Society, Baltimore, Md.: (1) The first fire mark of this company, issued in 1794, was handmade of tile on wood. No specimen of this mark has been found. (2) Issued about 1795. The iron casting of the clasped hands is mounted on the original wooden plaque. (3) Issued about 1820; iron casting on a wooden plaque. Index finger on the hand is much longer than in any other marks put out by this company. Cuffs are more pronounced and lacy than in the issue of 1795. Probably many valuable specimens were lost in the great Baltimore fire of 1904.

Mutual Insurance Company of Washington County, Hagerstown, Md.: (1) Issued in 1847. Iron casting, oblong with raised border. Shows hands clasped and raised initials of company.

Associated Firemen's Insurance Company of Baltimore, Md.: (1) Issued in 1848; of cast iron with rounded oval edge, very large and heavy. Mark shows a fireman blowing a horn and holding a burning brand.

Firemen's Insurance Company of Baltimore, Md.: (1) Mark, issued about 1840. Wheels of pumper have twelve spokes. Loop at top for hanging is plain. (2) Largest mark, issued about 1855. Loop at top for hanging is plain and round. Wheels of pumper have six spokes.

Firemen's Insurance Company of the District of Columbia: (1) Issued about 1838. Large, thick, iron casting, very heavy. Very similar to mark of the Firemen's of Baltimore, above.

Hartford County Mutual Fire Insurance Company: (1) Issued in 1831; made of tin, it is oval and convex.

Clay Fire and Marine Insurance Company, Newport, Ky.: (1) Issued in 1789; odd-shaped, iron casting.

Associated Firemen's Insurance Company of Pittsburgh, Pa.: (1) Issued about 1851; cast iron, showing a standing figure of a fireman, fully equipped, blowing a horn. In his left hand is a wrench for tapping the fire plug.

Penn Fire Insurance Company of Pittsburgh, Pa.: (1) Issued in 1841; it is of cast iron, showing the bust of William Penn.

Firemen's Insurance Company of Pittsburgh, Pa.: (1) Issued in 1834; it is an oblong, iron casting showing an old fire engine.

Western Mutual Fire and Marine Insurance Company, St. Louis, Mo.: (1) Issued in 1857; oval mark, showing clasped hands and name of company in raised letters.

Franklin Insurance Company, St. Louis, Mo.: (1) Issued in 1855; made of zinc. Has the name of the company and city on it.

Laclede Mutual Insurance Company, St. Louis, Mo.: (1) Issued in 1859; small, oval, tin mark. Light in weight, name of company in raised letters, clasped hands in center.

Washington Mutual Insurance Company, Boston, Mass.: (1) Issued in 1844; made of brass, oblong with raised border. Size 8½″ x 4¼″.

Protection Mutual Fire Insurance Company, Thomaston, Maine: (1) Issued in 1849; an oval, tin plate with the company's initials shown.

Insurance Company of Florida, Jacksonville, Fla.: (1) Issued in 1841; entirely of wood. Bears the letters "I.F." in high relief.

Mutual Assurance Company of New York City: (1) Issued 1787; of heavy tin, oval in shape. Painted black with "Mutual Assurance" in gilt letters. Number of the policy on a space beneath. (Only two specimens are extant today.)

Niagara District Mutual Fire Insurance Company, Niagara Falls, N.Y.: (1) Issued in 1836; a small, heavy, iron casting with very prominently raised, clasped hands. The name of the company runs around the edge of the mark, forming a border. Date of founding of company is also given.

Milwaukee Mechanics', Milwaukee, Wis.: (1) Issued in 1853; oval, iron casting with beaded edge, name of company showing plainly on front in raised letters.

Home Insurance Company, New Haven, Conn.: (1) Company lasted from 1859 to 1871. The fire mark is a thick, iron casting of oval shape. It shows the figure of a fireman and an old-time fire engine ,and plug in bold relief.

Protection Fire Insurance Company, Charleston, W.Va.: (1) Exact date of the organization of this company is not known; it went out of business in 1894 and undoubtedly was an old company. The mark is an oblong, iron casting showing raised eagle and name of company. A few years ago a large portion of Charleston was destroyed by fire, and many of these marks were lost.

Citizens' Fire, Marine and Life Insurance Company, Wheeling, W.Va.: (1) Issued in 1856; very odd-shaped casting, with name of company in raised letters.

Peabody Fire and Marine Insurance Company, Wheeling, West Va.: (1) Issued in 1869; a heavy, iron casting; fancy, oblong shape.

Perhaps, if you are lucky, you will find a fire mark similar to the ones described above or even another design which is even rarer and which might be in the $1,000 bracket.

XXIX

DEAD WHALES, HAIR NETS—AND A
DASH OF BEAUTY

Women's Follies through the Ages

A WOMAN will do anything to enhance her beauty, even if it
means wading out into the ocean to drag in the contents of
the intestinal canal of a dead whale.

Each year more and more treasure seekers scour long stretches
of our beaches trying to locate the gray smelly substance that is
ambergris. Most of the time the substance found is nothing more
than vegetable wax or soap from passing ships, but the one find in a
thousand will be the gray lumps which are ambergris—that fantastic substance so necessary for the retention of the delicate odors
of perfumes—without which perfume would be of little use to the
woman who treasures it so highly.

The smell of ambergris, as found in the ocean—if you are lucky
enough to find it—has been likened both to musk and to a sweet
earthy odor. Often it will contain the beaks of cuttlefish, and this is
one way of telling whether or not the substance you have found is
actually ambergris—or somebody's left-over soap.

Usually found in small amounts, it sometimes appears as a great
glob weighing as much as five hundred pounds!

In ancient days, ambergris was used for medicinal purposes and
was purported to be the excrement of the sperm whale. Today we
know that at its origin the ambergris is enclosed in the intestinal

158

canal of the sperm whale. Also, it *must* come from a diseased whale. It is for this reason that ambergris is so rare. One whale is capable of producing hundreds of pounds of this substance, but, then, how many sick whales are there?

It is this scarcity of ambergris which makes the price paid for it so high—in recent years reaching about $20 a pound, or $2,000 per one hundred pounds, or $10,000 for five hundred pounds. Obviously well worth watching for—and even wading for.

Yet there are other items connected with perfume that can be found without getting your feet wet. Among them the cones which were set into the wigs worn by the women of ancient Egypt. These cones contained perfume and would, today, be considered items of great historical interest.

The Romans also had their own methods of filling the air with scent. The women of Rome carried silver and golden nets into which were placed small balls of amber, and when the amber was rubbed, it threw off fragrance into the air—amber balls worth watching for.

Besides perfume, there are other treasures used by women of the past to enhance their beauty, and among them are examples of embroidery.

There have been times in our history when embroidery ranked as high in prestige as the great paintings of the day. Some examples of this ancient art have survived—and they may be waiting for you to find them. From ancient China, watch for the silk, brocade-embroidered robes of the women who lived under the ancient Manchus. Watch for the white robes of the ancient Greeks, robes embroidered in reds, blues, yellows, and other colors.

In earlier times, during the Middle Ages, embroidery was so popular that monasteries and convents had special rooms where nothing else was done except that work. The patterns showed a Byzantine influence—fine and lovely workmanship for the treasure hunter to locate, if he can.

From the thirteen to the fifteen hundreds, Europe was a center for some of the most exquisite pieces of embroidered work the world had ever known, lovely things to clothe the most beautiful ladies of the land.

Even the men got into the embroidery act, in the seventeen hundreds, when Louis XV ruled France and it was fashionable for men of the court to appear in handsomely embroidered coats. These coats are today well worth your search, keeping in mind that some of the most beautiful of these had been sent all the way to China for their embroidery work—although the design of the embroidery was distinctly European.

Rarity, age, historical association, and fine workmanship are the criteria upon which is based the evaluation of any piece of embroidery. Let us hope that the piece of embroidery which has been in your family for so many years can meet the rigid standards of these pieces of worked cloth which are considered as great art in their own right.

But embroidery is not the only cloth to watch for, beautiful though it is. Ancient Japanese brocade robes dating to the late 1500's would be museum pieces if you could find good examples of them. Also from ancient Japan come robes which were decorated with gold and silver foil, sometimes even with glass. How heavy these must have been for the women who wore them, especially since the Japanese ladies wore as many as twenty articles of dress at once, one over the other.

From ancient Byzantium, watch for cloth of gold. They wore fantastic garments, from patterned silk to cloth, into which gold was woven; many of them are museum pieces.

In feudal times, the noble ladies of the land wore cloth woven with gold. They called it aureotextile. Sometimes they wore aureoclavi, which means brocaded with gold. Women's clothing from this period is always worth watching for, especially since it became so fabulous that laws were passed limiting the extravagances to which women might go in having their clothes decorated.

From the later period of the Renaissance there are many items of clothing to watch for—brocades and velvets and silks. Robes were lined with crimson silk, or sometimes with ermine and sable.

Fashion was so important at one time that fashion dolls were made especially to display the latest thing in milady's fashion world. This was in the late thirteen hundreds, when each year the city of Venice sent to Paris for a fashion doll which, on Ascension Day, was placed on display in Piazza San Marco.

Whether it is a fashion doll, a piece of golden embroidery, or a gray and smelly lump of ambergris, it is treasure—if you can find it.

TRULY the beauty of womankind offers an unlimited field to the treasure hunter, since there are almost no limits to the length to which women have gone in the past—and probably will in the future—to enhance their charms, and probably the most familiar of these aids to beauty is the necklace.

Rubies, diamonds, emeralds, gold, and silver, have gone into the baubles which have encircled the necks of some of the world's most famous beauties. These necklaces of the past are well within the scope of the treasure hunter. Whether they are very ancient or comparatively modern—provided they are of fine craftsmanship or set with precious stones or can be proven to have belonged to some particularly important personage.

The necklaces of ancient Egypt were of exceptionally fine quality —and certainly are worth the treasure hunter's time. Necklaces of this period have already been found, of course; one of these finds being a serpent necklace discovered on the mummy of the royal Egyptian princess, Knoumit. The necklace was of gold, silver, and emeralds. This, naturally, was a tremendous find—but there are other Egyptian necklaces which have never been located. And, since many of the ancient combs were desecrated and robbed and the items found therein scattered to all parts of the world, there is really no telling where you might find another treasure similar to the necklace of Princess Knoumit.

Also watch for the necklaces of ancient Crete. The British Museum already has examples of these fine necklaces, of amethyst, rock crystal, and carnelian beads, but there were others which may never be found—and others which may be found by you.

The necklaces of ancient Persia should also not be forgotten. One of the greatest finds was made near Susa in the early part of the twentieth century when Henry de Morgan discovered a sarcophagus. It contained the skeleton of a woman, and with her skeleton were many necklaces—emerald and jade and turquoise and lapis lazuli. There was also one other necklace, a three-row necklace of pearls. Originally it had consisted of over four hundred pearls, and when de Morgan found the necklace, over two hundred of the pearls were still in good condition. Who knows what other necklaces are still hidden from the eyes of mankind—waiting to be found by a treasure hunter.

With the amount of grave robbing through the ages there is no telling what you might find—anywhere—whether it is in the bazaars of the east or even here in America. Tourists have brought back stranger things than lost treasures, without even knowing what they had.

One of the objects to keep in mind—and certainly they were on the minds of beautiful women of the past—are brooches, such as the medieval brooches of the Irish and the Anglo-Saxon women. But these are not the only brooches to watch for. There are brooches from all times and all eras—from the plain and simple historic brooches to those which are of value because of their precious-stone settings.

Nor did the beauties of the past neglect their arms. They decorated them with some of the most magnificent bracelets the world has ever seen. In the time of ancient Egypt, all kinds of precious stones and enamels were used to make beautiful bracelets.

Some of these ancient Egyptian bracelets have already been found, among them the bracelets of the Queen of Zer. These are of gold and turquoise, and at least one of them is decorated with golden hawks.

There were other bracelets—those of the Persians, the Medes, the ancient Jews, and the ancient Greeks of the time of the Trojan War. All worth watching for.

Gold powder is another item to look for from this era. This, however, was used by the men of ancient Persia, who actually dusted their long, curled beards with gold powder.

Gold powder for dusting the beard may seem unusual to us, but it certainly is not as unusual, nor as beautiful, as some of the decorations of the women of long ago—all of which are listed as treasure-hunting items.

Among these must be included the forehead jewels used by the women of the Renaissance. These gems were worn in the middle of the forehead, sometimes attached to a head veil. These were beautiful then and are beautiful today—if you can find them.

These treasures of women's beauty can be found by anyone, even by a farmer who found a ring and tied it to his dog's collar. The dog wore it for over six months—until the farmer discovered that the ring was gold. It turned out that the ring had belonged to Ethelswith, sister of Alfred the Great, Queen of Mercia in the ninth century. Today this ring is a prized possession of the British Museum.

Another famous find was made in a field at Stratford-on-Avon, when the ring that Anne Hathaway allegedly gave to William Shakespeare was discovered.

The value of a ring, if you find one, is increased a great deal if it belonged to a famous person—or if the ring is set with precious stones so that it has a value of itself. But whether the ring you find is a golden ring of Mycenae, an English iconographic gold and silver ring bearing images of the Saints and made in the 15th century, an antique memorial ring, or a unique and ancient ring of any kind, it is worth while having it examined by an expert. At least don't attach it to your dog's collar.

From rings to fingernails is not a long step in beauty adornment —as the women of ancient China proved with their Manchu finger guards. These guards, protecting the long fingernails which were a sign of class status, were made of silver and gold and jade.

Whatever it is that you find, have it checked. If it was used to beautify a woman and if it is set with diamonds or emeralds or rubies, your problems are solved—no matter what famous person may have worn it. But sometimes it takes a little more to make an item of jewelry into a treasure. Such as the hairwork jewelry which was so popular during the 1800's. Made of human hair, these were bracelets, earrings, and charms for charm bracelets. Originally, hairwork jewelry was a kind of keepsake, made from the hair of a loved one who had died. But as time went on it became a fad and there was hardly anyone who did not have at least one item of hairwork jewelry. Today hairwork jewelry has a minimal value.

For example, hairwork brooches and earrings can be purchased for from $50 to $100. But, if you find examples of hairwork jewelry which had belonged to a famous person, or if the jewelry itself has an unusual history, the value of the item would naturally increase. And this is a point to remember when looking for any items used by women from time immemorial to enhance their beauty.

XXX

EAT, DRINK, AND BE MERRY

Silver, China, Spoons

CRAFTSMEN of all the ages have catered to man's necessities, and because of this the treasure hunter can search his attics, his cellars, and the second-hand stores for treasures unimaginable.

Dishes that look like junk, battered teapots, little figurines to make your tables and your rooms look prettier, silver of all kinds— all these you can find and all of them are worth money in your pocket if you will only look for them.

Silver of any kind if it was made by Paul Revere is valuable—if you can find it. Collectors and museum curators will always bid eagerly for it, paying thousands of dollars for even a goblet made by him.

One man owned a Revere goblet but thought it was only junk. However, he called in dealers to look at it. The first one offered him the current price for silver by the ounce, but the second dealer recognized it as Revere and paid him over $4,000 for it.

This does not mean that the first dealer was dishonest, but it does show that even experts can overlook lost treasures because they do not look closely enough or because they do not know which treasures are missing and therefore valuable.

These missing treasures of Paul Revere can be anywhere! A missing Revere copperplate, the one on which Massachusetts shillings were printed in 1775, was found in a junk pile in Scotland. Today it rests with the Antiquarian Society in Worcester.

How far a treasure can travel before the discerning eye of the treasure hunter spots it for what it is! Much of our early American silver, including Revere silver, was sent to England in the early days by families who remained loyal to the Crown. But much of it is still in America. Some of it is in the museums—but some of it is hiding in America's attics, waiting for the treasure hunter to find it.

On the other hand, some of the English items were sent to America. Tea caddies of this period, for example, worth from only a few dollars to several hundred dollars apiece, depending of course on age, condition, rarity, maker, etc.

The ever popular Toby jugs should be on every treasure hunter's list, for they are on every collector's list. Worth from a few dollars to $100 or more apiece, they can still be found—if you are willing to look for them.

Even the round, three-footed, cooking pots used by our ancestors in their open fireplaces can be worth something—if you will take the time to locate them.

However, in looking for American silver, caddies, and three-footed cooking pots, do not neglect items of European older make which are missing, such as the fabled Medici china!

In the late fifteen and the early sixteen hundreds Medici china —bowls, plates, vases, etc.—was made in Florence, Italy, and to-day there are not even fifty pieces of this magnificent china in existence—that is, unless you can find it.

Any piece of this china would truly be found treasure if you could locate it. There is no museum in the world that would not want it.

But not everyone can find Medici china. So try for Staffordshire china, made in Staffordshire and slanted toward the Pennsylvania Dutch market. Pieces of Staffordshire are rare, because in the past collectors thought very little of them and they were allowed to be lost or destroyed. Today they are not only desired but sought after by the collectors, who are more than willing to pay for whatever you can find. A piece of Staffordshire can be worth over $100—if you are lucky enough to find it. I have even seen prices quoted as high as $1,800 for one piece of rare Staffordshire.

Also watch for Lowestoft china, a rare piece of which can be worth hundreds of dollars. A rare but complete set of Lowestoft can be worth a couple of thousand—at least.

A set of Worcester china, if complete, can also be valuable. A complete set can be worth over $1,000—if complete, fine enough, and rare enough.

Also watch for Crown Derby china, any of it. If you are lucky enough you will find a rare piece, or if you are very lucky, a complete set.

Historical interest and not monetary value alone is sometimes important. There is also the excitement of finding important missing items, like the dessert service of flowers and blue and gold, with the mark "S," which belonged to George Washington. Only three pieces are known to be extant today—unless you can find the rest of them.

There is also a set of plates decorated with an eagle and initialed "G." and "M. W." for George and Martha Washington. Only one of these plates is known to be in existence. The others are lost—unless you can find them. Nor can any value be placed on Washington's missing china, until someone finds it. Perhaps it will bring a great deal and perhaps very little, depending on its condition and how badly the collectors want it.

Anything which comes out of the dining rooms or the kitchens of yesteryear can have some value, however—even if it did not belong to a president. Even such odd-sounding things as spiders and trivets have some value. Spiders and trivets are both names for a metal stand used to hold hot kettles. Used in front of fireplaces as early as the 1600's, they are today collectors' items.

Or perhaps you might find lusterware, each piece worth $50 or so—depending on condition, age, etc.—or some of the gold work of the early colonies, or Sheffield plate, which is in such demand by collectors.

Or you might find early pewter ware—items which always sell to collectors. Or, if you are very lucky, rare Chinese porcelain, sometimes worth a great deal if it is old enough, rare enough, and in fine enough condition.

Or you might find figurines, some of them worth only a few dollars, some of them worth $1,000 or more.

Any old silver, old china, or anything made for the comfort and beauty of the dining rooms and kitchens of the past has some value.

Even spoons have value, and one kind of valuable spoon is the apostle spoon! Collectors vie for these apostle spoons, which were made during the Middle Ages and which were still being made as late as the sixteenth century. Souvenirs of the birth of a child, these spoons would be presented as gifts at the christening.

Spoons were so rare at that time that when a person went visiting he was expected to bring his own—if he was wealthy enough to have one in the first place.

To give out apostle spoons made of silver was a mark of good breeding, fine birth, and social standing, in the Middle Ages, since only the wealthy could afford spoons of any kind.

The Middle Ages were filled with superstitions and not the least of these was the one that silver could drive out disease. For this reason, when a baby was born to a wealthy family, the parents had a silver spoon placed in his mouth to protect the child against illness. From this comes the expression "To be born with a silver spoon in the mouth" which even today means to be born of wealthy parents. For only the wealthy could afford a silver spoon and only the very wealthy could afford to give away apostle spoons as christening gifts.

Each of these latter spoons was dedicated to a particular apostle, and the finial [a decoration at the top of its handle] of each spoon showed a likeness of one of the apostles.

A full set of apostle spoons would consist of twelve, although occasionally there would be an extra spoon picturing Christ, and sometimes there would also be a spoon representing the Virgin.

Only one complete set of apostle spoons, all of them of the same date, is known to be in existence today. Dated 1628, this set is in the Goldsmith's Hall in London. It consists of thirteen spoons, because it includes the extra one representative of the "Master."

Even one apostle spoon is of some value—but if you should find a complete set and all of the same date, remember that only one other complete set exists today.

Whether it is china, silver or gold—if it belonged in the dining rooms and the kitchens of yesterday—it belongs in the museums of today.

XXXI

Paper Fortunes

Rare Stamps

IF there is a businessman who doubts the advisability of collecting stamps, it might be well to quote him a price brought in the recent auction of one of the great stamp collections.

The collection was so large that it was sold in sixteen different phases. The total stamps and covers had brought in $2,895,146. In any language this spells big business.

Part of this big business can be the treasure hunter's—if he knows what to look for!

Like the twenty-four-cent airmail issue of 1918. Each of the stamps of this issue is worth around $4,000—and there are thirteen of them missing. If you find one, look at the airplane in the corner. It is upside down.

Or watch for examples of the postmasters' provisionals, which were issued between March 3, 1845, the date on which Congress determined on rates of postage, and March 3, 1847, the date on which Congress determined that the Postmaster General should issue stamps.

Between these two dates the local postmasters issued their own stamps. These are the provisionals, which can make a fortune for you—if you can find them.

Watch for provisionals from such places as St. Louis, Mo.; Alexandria, Va.; New Haven, Conn.; Annapolis, Md.; Millbury, Mass.; Baltimore, Md.; Lockport, N.Y.; Boscawen, N.H.; Brattleboro, Vt., and New York, N.Y. Prices for provisional stamps and envelopes from these cities can range from a few dollars to $15,000, depending on condition, etc.

If you are lucky enough, you might find stamps worth thousands —just by remembering what to look for.

Stamp collecting is not just a hobby—it has become a national pastime. Today, in America, there are more than ten million stamp collectors. If you find a stamp, there is a buyer for it somewhere in America.

Remember, however, that with stamps, condition is the most important factor. To get a good price a stamp must be in fine condition. Also, if possible, retain the envelope. Often, the addition of the original envelope raises the value of the stamp.

Watch for any early stamp, and remember that it has not been too many years since the whole idea of postage stamps started.

Early stamps, stamps with errors in them, are all worth watching for. However, only the experts can tell whether or not a stamp is valuable. You can get some idea from stamp catalogues, but only the expert can tell whether or not the stamp you have is exactly the same and is in good enough condition to warrant the high values listed in the catalogues.

Also keep in mind the possible variation between the opinions of the experts. One stamp which I know about was valued by one expert at $1,000. Another expert valued the stamp at $750 and still another expert placed its value between $35 and $50.

If you have a stamp which you think might be valuable, take it to several experts and get all of their opinions. Needless to say, the thing to do then is to sell to the highest bidder.

Anyone can find a stamp. It takes no training or experience or courage, as some of the more adventuresome lost treasures do, such as the hidden pirate treasures or sunken ships. And you do not need to travel to find stamps. They could be anywhere—in your attic, in your basement, or stuck between the pages of a book.

Look again at any old envelope which you might find. Look through the old boxes you see at neighborhood auctions. It does not matter where you look; everyone has seen old letters and old envelopes lying around—and thrown them away thoughtlessly—and no one knows how many thousands of dollars worth of stamps have been destroyed or incinerated when disposing of "that old junk."

It might help in recognizing valuable stamps, if you can attend some of the stamp shows which are held from time to time in almost every town of any size in America. Look at the stamps on display which have value—and remember them. Buy a catalogue and check every odd or strange stamp against the displays on its pages.

Watch for errors. Sometimes, though not always, the fact that an error appears on a stamp indicates that it is valuable, and it is at least a good indication that the stamp might have value.

Above all, remember the rarest of the American stamps, among which are the twenty-four-cent airmail of 1918 with the upside down airplane and the postmasters' provisionals. Any early stamp can have value—like the 1869 fifteen-cent stamp with an upside down picture, which can be worth as high as $10,000. Or the 1869 thirty-cent stamp which has inverted flags in its design. This one can be valued as high as $8,000.

Prices, of course, depend upon age, rarity, right issue, etc., but there are so many stamps worth a great deal of money that it would be impossible to enumerate them all here.

Just remember that there is a fortune in those little pieces of paper you see on envelopes every day of the year—if you can find the right ones.

There are missing stamps which are worth $100,000 apiece—if you can find them. These are the fabled British Guianas.

Issued in 1856, these stamps are square. On the front appears a four-word inscription, easily identified if you find one.

Strangely enough, however, the best-known copy of the stamp has had its corners clipped off. And there is another strange fact about this extant British Guiana: no one knows who owns it! The possessor of the stamp wishes to remain anonymous. There was a time when rumors flew thick and fast about the stamp having been a gift to President Roosevelt, one of our most famous stamp collectors.

The President denied the rumor, and the identity of the owner still remains a mystery! Originally this unique stamp was located by a schoolboy, who sold it to an English dealer for five shillings! The stamp, however, did not rest here—or at this value. It was sold and sold again until it became a part of the world-famous Ferrary collection.

Yet once more the stamp moved on. It was willed to the Berlin Postal Museum and because of this the French government confiscated it. At that time funds were needed to finance the reparation debt of the Germans, and the French placed the British Guiana on the auction block.

Present at this now famous auction were two men, a M. Burrus, a French tobacco merchant, and Arthur Hind, an American manufacturer. Tension filled the room as other bidders fell by the wayside until only the bidding of Hinds and M. Burrus could be heard.

In total silence the bidding went higher and higher, and, when the price had reached $32,500, Hinds, the American, had won. He walked out of that auction the owner of one of the rarest stamps in the world.

He kept the British Guiana for the rest of his life, and, when he died, his wife placed it in the hands of an American stamp store. They sold it for an undisclosed price rumored to be more than $45,000.

The man who bought it now has a stamp valued at $100,000; yet, like many collectors, he remains anonymous, his name undisclosed to the public.

In his hands, anonymous though he is, is this copy of one of the rarest stamps in the world—yet there is a chance you might find another one if you look hard enough at those old envelopes in the attic trunk or in that old box of papers in the basement. You might even find it in an envelope stuck between the pages of a book as a marker. Certainly stranger things have happened in the world of philately.

The British Guiana, however, is not the only stamp to watch for. There are, for example, the Mauritius one- and two-penny stamps which are inscribed with the words "Post Office" instead of "Post Paid."

Just one of these Mauritius stamps has a value of approximately $20,000, depending on condition, etc. One collector is lucky enough to be in possession of an envelope which bears two of the Mauritius stamps. This envelope with its precious stamps is valued at $75,000.

Maybe you might be this lucky—if you look hard enough for one of these stamps which were originally issued at the direct order of a

Governor's wife. Lady Gomm needed stamps with which she might frank party invitations—and so the Mauritius one- and two-penny stamps were issued.

The stamps, however, carried an error. Where the engraver should have put "Post Paid" he put "Post Office." The error was eventually corrected, but stamps that contain the error are now listed as being among the most valuable stamps in the world —worth approximately $20,000 apiece.

There are also other stamps which can reach this value! Such as the "Missionaries," which range in value from $2,000 to $20,000, depending upon the original value of the stamp (two-cent, three-cent, etc.) and upon its condition.

These stamps were issued in the Hawaiian Islands and were called "Missionaries" obviously because the people who made the most use of them were missionaries. And they are listed as among the rarest stamps in the world—and therefore should be among the first of the stamps for the treasure hunter to watch for.

Also watch for the Swiss Cantonal stamps issued between 1843 and 1850, stamps which are ranked high in the list of most-wanted stamps.

D ID you know that there are Confederate stamps which are worth fortunes?

There are many of these rare and valuable stamps to be found on envelopes dating from the Civil War, stuck in an old desk or hidden in great-great-grandma's trunk. Certain "rebel" stamps are today considered to be among the most valuable in the philatelic world despite the fact that most Confederate stamps can today be bought for practically nothing. The Confederate government printed many stamps and today most of them are interesting to us only historically. Only a certain few have attained the status of rare stamps. They are the Confederate provisionals.

These stamps may be found hand-stamped or press-printed on many kinds of envelopes—symbol, perhaps, of a south at war. They may be found on commercial as well as homemade envelopes. Sometimes these homemade envelopes were made of maps, printed forms, or even wallpaper.

If you have a stamp on an envelope, however, that envelope should show postmarks of the town of issue. Local postmasters in the south had answered the need for **Confe**derate stamps by issuing their own between June 1 and October 14, 1861. These stamps issued through the necessity of war are called the confederate provisionals.

Provisionals were printed wherever proper workmen and materials were available. Everyone who could print, it seems, wanted to get into the act.

On June 1, 1861, the south stopped using the stamps made by the Yankee government. It was not, however, until October 14 of that same year that their own confederate stamps appeared. It was, therefore, necessary to obtain stamps from somewhere to keep communications open. So the local towns and cities made their own. These are the Confederate Provisionals.

The states had seceded from the Union, men drew swords to fight their brothers—and Abraham Lincoln served as President!

Bitterness reigned and ripped apart a nation. There were big problems but there were also little ones! For example! How do you mail a letter without having to use a hated Yankee stamp?

J. H. Reagan, a Texan, was the confederate postmaster-general and he urgently needed workers for his new post office. By the simple expedient of writing to the Yankee post office in Washington and asking a number of clerks in the post office department there if they would not much rather work for the confederacy, he got his staff. All but two of the gentlemen accepted!

It was Mr. Reagan who set the June first date as the last day on which the southerners would use the Yankee stamp. All postmasters had to render their accounts as of that date. On the same day the postmaster-general of the Union suspended Yankee postal service in the south.

By October 14, proper Confederate stamps were available for use, yet even after this date, sometimes, these Confederate provisionals were used when the supply of regular stamps ran out.

These Confederate provisionals today bring in value "what the market will bear." But at the same time there are certain price ranges wherein a stamp may fall. A stamp is valuable depending on its rarity, its condition, and the desirability it has for the buyer. Its value can depend on many things. That is one reason why no set value can be placed on a stamp; yet it is certain that you should keep an eye out for Confederate provisional stamps and envelopes from:

Athens, Georgia; Autaugaville, Alabama.
Baton Rouge, Louisiana; Beaumont, Texas; Bridgeville, Alabama.
Danville, Virginia.
Emory, Virginia.
Franklin, North Carolina.
Goliad, Texas; Gonzales, Texas; Greenville, Alabama; Grove Hill, Alabama.
Helena, Texas.
Jetersville, Virginia.
Knoxville, Tennessee.
Lenoir, North Carolina; Livingston, Alabama.
Macon, Georgia; Marion, Virginia; Mt. Lebanon, Louisiana.
New Smyrna, Florida.
Pittsylvania C.H., Virginia; Pleasant Shade, Virginia.
Salem, Virginia; Liberty, Virginia; Salisbury, North Carolina; Spartanburg, South Carolina.
Uniontown, Alabama.
Victoria, Texas.

Prices for some of the above stamps range from $1,000 to $15,000 apiece, depending on the original face value of the stamp, condition, etc. Of course there are more locales of this period which also issued valuable stamps but which are not listed, so if you have any southern stamp dated between June 1 and October 14, 1861, have it checked by a competent authority.

XXXII

ANYTHING THAT GLITTERS

Topaz, Amber, Pearls, Gold, Emeralds and Jade

A TEXAS rancher found a blue topaz weighing approximately seven hundred carats! This was many years ago at a spot near Mason, Texas.

Not too long ago, in Mason County, also in Texas, three men searched and worked for three days to make a topaz "find." Finally, tired and discouraged, they gave up. They put their equipment back in the car convinced that luck was against them. Yet, one woman along on the hunt decided to take a walk—and found a blue topaz weighing over two hundred carats!

A topaz can be valuable if it is a perfect stone. Finding a perfect topaz can be a lucky thing for the treasure hunter even in modern times, although in ancient times the hunter had an even more important reason to hunt topaz than we do. For the topaz not only had monetary value. It had the supposed power to avert sudden death!

In the United States we have found colorless, blue, yellow, and sherry-brown topaz. And there are more to be found—if you know where to look.

Watch for topaz at Mason County, Texas; at Topsham, Maine; at Nathrop and the Tarryall Mountains north of Lake George in Colorado; in the Thomas Mountain district of Utah, and in San Diego County, California.

Almost everywhere there is some sort of bauble to watch for—

even the organically fossilized gum on extinct trees, such as amber, a good sized lump of which can be worth as high as $1,000.

Watch for amber in Richmond County, New York; Cape Sable, Maryland; Mercer, Salem and Camden Counties, New Jersey; and in Dukes County, Massachusetts.

Also, while you are watching for topaz and amber, do not forget the pearl. You do not need to go to exotic isles or foreign shores to find pearls. You can look for them right here in your own backyard.

Precious pearls can and have been found in America. They are produced by Quadrula, a fresh-water mussel. Chances are, of course, that the fresh-water pearls you find will not have the same value as marine pearls, but fresh-water types can be precious pearls.

Watch for them in the rivers of Michigan and Wisconsin. Try the Mississippi Valley, Tennessee, Iowa and Arkansas. Watch for them in Kentucky, New Jersey and Illinois.

Way back in the 1850's a farmer was chasing a cow. His foot struck a rock which, with the impact of his foot, broke off; when he stopped to look at it he saw that it was spotted with gold. Another discovery had been made, and, before it was over, over $1,000,000 in gold had been taken out of the spot where the farmer had stumbled over the rock. And only a hundred and fifty feet away they took $4,000,000 worth of gold out of the ground!

Anyone who vacations has a chance to find gold by panning in the stream beds of the gold country. Even the boy scout on a camping trip can come home with gold. All he needs is his gold pan, a little luck—and a little knowledge.

The yellow of gold is known to everyone. To find gold in a stream is an easy thing. When you see it, you know it, instinctively. It may be shaped as a grain, a nugget or sometimes fine as sand. But it is gold.

When you are not sure of what you have, or you just want to know for sure, write to the United States Department of the Interior, Washington, D.C. They have information on gems and minerals—and if they do not have the information you want, they can tell you who to ask. However, do *not* ship them your samples of gems or gold, just *ask* for information.

There are also local gem and rock clubs for you to contact. Almost any town of any size has one of these clubs, and the members are almost always kind and courteous and willing to help.

Also write to the United States Government Printing Office, Washington 25, D.C., asking for a list of the booklets they print pertaining to gems, etc. These pamphlets are sold to the general public for a minimum fee and they contain some of the finest and most complete information.

Remember, anything that glitters is worth at least an investigation. With a rockhound's pick, a gold mining pan (even an old pie pan will work in an emergency) and the help of the United States Government, you might come home from your vacation with a fortune!

I F you can find an emerald which is of good quality and large in size (over six carats), its value would be greater than that of a diamond.

The dark green of the emerald is among the most beautiful sights on earth, especially to the finder. To find a stone of gem quality is a very rare thing, though emeralds have been found in the United States. In North Carolina there are so-called emerald mines in several areas, but they are not active. There have also been reports of emerald finds along the Bowen River in South Carolina.

It is possible that you might be the one who finds an emerald within the United States—possibly along the banks of the Bowen River. And certainly if you could spot the superb grass green of a large gem emerald, its value would be great. The grass green of the emerald is a magnificent green—but there is only one true imperial green. This is the imperial green of jade, the green which is the most highly prized although jade comes in all shades of green.

We always think of jade as being associated only with the Orient; yet not too many years ago a huge jade boulder weighing over one thousand pounds was found in California near the area of the Trinity River. The boulder was one solid mass of every shade of green imaginable—and some of it was thought to be imperial green. And in Mendocino County, California, a large deposit of jade was found.

Jade, in both varieties, jadeite and nephrite, ranges in colors from white to dark green, but the imperial green jade is the most highly desired. A necklace of matched imperial beads has been valued at $100,000.

The finding of just one piece of jade can turn family picnics into

wild scrambles in search for more. Watch for both nephrite and
jadeite—although jadeite is rarer and therefore has more value. But
watch for both of them along the beaches and in stream beds, and
also watch for deposits of jade.

Watch for the rare jadeite at the North Fork of the Eel River,
Trinity County, California; Clear Creek, San Benito County and in
Cloverdale and Valley Ford, Sonoma County, California.

Watch for nephrite at the North Fork of the Eel River, Trinity
County, California; southeast of Lander, Wyoming; and Marin,
Monterey and Tulare Counties, California.

The West seems to have all the best of it when it comes to jade
hunting, but in North Carolina they have found rubies. Everyone
knows the value of the ruby, especially the prized pigeon's blood
color. The deep, deep red of the most highly prized rubies defies
description, and the value of a fine ruby is higher than that of a
diamond—if you can find it.

Watch for gem-quality rubies in stream beds and stream gravels
especially. Watch for them at Cowee Valley, Macon County, North
Carolina; and at Yogo Creek, Judith Basin County, Montana. Also
watch for them in both Wyoming and Colorado. In Wyoming, gem
rubies have been found at Marion Claim, Fremont County; in Colorado, they have been found at the Calumet mine, Salida.

If you should discover a gem similar to a ruby but which is some
other color, and especially if it is a cornflower blue, do not throw it
away. It may not be a ruby—but it could be a sapphire. Both rubies
and sapphires are corundum—and both are worth your search. The
red is ruby—but sapphire can be pink, green or yellow, salmon,
cornflower blue, or colorless.

Watch for sapphires in Montana at Dry Cottonwood Creek deposit, northeast of Butte, Deer Lodge County; the Rock Creek
deposit southwest of Philipsburg, Granite County; Missouri River
deposits, northeast of Helena; Quartz Gulch, in Granite County;
also in Chouteau County; Pole Creek, Madison County, and Browns
Gulch, Silver Bow County.

Watch for sapphires in Indiana in Morgan County. In Idaho,
watch for them in Washington and Adams Counties. Look for them
in Colorado in Fremont County, and in California at Barstow, San
Bernardino County.

Sapphires have also been found at the Calumet iron mine in

Chaffee County, Colorado, and at the Corundum Hill mine, Macon County, North Carolina, and the Sapphire and White Water mine, Jackson County, North Carolina.

You might find a cornflower blue, that most prized sapphire! Buried in the anonymous rocks of a river deposit, or coated so with dirt that unless luck is with you, you might pass it by.

This almost happened to one of the world's most famous gemstones, the Australian Andamooks Opal, now belonging to Elizabeth of England. The gem is now magnificently set as the main stone of a necklace with matching earrings. But, originally, the opal, over four inches long and two inches wide in the rough, was so dirty that not even the miners recognized it for what it was until one of them accidentally chipped it with his pick.

So if, here in America, you chance across a dirty stone but which, if you look closely, shimmers and dances with inner fires, hang on to it. It could be opal—for opal too has been found here in America.

In the state of Nevada there is a place called Virgin Valley, where at some time in the eons of the past barks of trees, pine cones, and driftwood were covered by volcanic ash. Today, if you look carefully enough, some of them have become opals.

This Virgin Valley is noted for its precious opal, the most valuable of the opal gems. Also look for precious opal in lava flows of the Columbia plateaus in Washington, Oregon and Idaho.

The so-called common opal, less rare and less valuable, can be found in Oregon, New York, Florida, New Jersey, Georgia and North Carolina.

The rarest of all the opals, of course, is the black opal, but more familiar to most of us are the white opals and the fire opals, aptly named because their inner flame resembles a rainbow fire unequalled in any other gem in the world.

The opal is known throughout the world as a "bad luck" stone, but certainly no treasure hunter would consider it bad luck to find a prize gem, an opal of fine quality. If he is extremely fortunate, however, he will find an emerald, a ruby, or a piece of imperial jade.

XXXIII

Razz-Ma-Tazz

Campaign Memorabilia

THE parades, the long-winded speeches, the songs, the hand-shaking, the razz-ma-tazz—these are the outward signs of an American political campaign, always a very special event in the life of the nation. Campaigns in the past were more flamboyant than they are today, and perhaps we treasure the memories of those former days for just that reason.

Mr. V. G. Stevens of Concord, Calif., is one of America's top collectors of campaign memorabilia. He has a collection of over two thousand items, which he has spent over thirty years in amassing.

Campaign items from before 1870 are, according to Mr. Stevens, "scarce and getting scarcer." He also states that Brown and Nixon pins and items should be saved, as there will come a day when they will be hard to find.

There is a pin with the name "Will" over a drawing of a key—who else but Wilkie? Wilkie-McNary and Dewey pins and memorabilia are also getting scarcer, according to Mr. Stevens.

The slogan "Full Dinner Pail" decorated the sides of the metal-and-glass pails that promoted the campaign of William McKinley, helping him to win the election. Slogans like "God Bless America," "Help Hoover Help Business," "Roosevelt and Relief," and "Wilkie and Work" abound on campaign mementoes.

Reminiscent of British cries of "Long live the King!" were the first Presidential items bearing the legend, "Long Live the President." The President, naturally, was George Washington.

According to Mr. Stevens, 1860 Lincoln items are very scarce, yet they are still occasionally found. A rare Lincoln campaign item, a portrait of Lincoln and Hamlin inset into a brass slug, was found not too long ago, in with some old buttons.

Modern campaign items commemorating the following men are collectors' items:

James Cox
John W. Davis
Eugene Debs
James C. Field
Franklin D. Roosevelt
James Weaver

Hunting for campaign items like the following is a fascinating pastime:

banners
beer steins
buttons
cane tops
cartoons
china
Currier and Ives prints
daguerreotypes
fabrics
fireplace tiles
gadgets
hats
kerosene torchlights
noisemakers
parasols
pictures
pins
plates
pottery
prints
sewing boxes
sheet music
snuff boxes
song sheets
statues
whiskey bottle corks
whiskey bottles

All of these are decorated with pictures, slogans or designs publicizing a political aspirant, his coworkers and/or his political party.

Presidential campaign buttons are desired, of course, but don't overlook campaign buttons for governor, senator, or any other political office. Also, those who tried unsuccessfully for the nomination during party conventions are still remembered by the collectors of campaign memorabilia. As it might be not so easy to recognize an item belonging to one of the also-rans, I am here adding a list of the men who ran for President of the United States and lost.

John Bell
James G. Blaine
William J. Bryan
Lewis Cass
Henry Clay
De Witt Clinton
James M. Cox
William H. Crawford
John W. Davis
Thomas E. Dewey
Stephen A. Douglas
John C. Fremont
Horace Greeley
Winfield S. Hancock
Charles E. Hughes
Rufus King
Robert M. LaFollette
Alfred Landon
George McClellan
Alton B. Parker
Charles Pinckney
Winfield Scott
Horatio Seymour
Alfred E. Smith
J. Strom Thurmond
Samuel J. Tilden
James Weaver
Wendell Wilkie

DO you have any old telephones up in the attic? They may have been yesterday's junk when they first became old, but today they are antiques. Types to watch for include almost all the older models, some of which date from the 1890's.

The old oak telephones are still fairly easy to find, but an old telephone with a solid walnut case is considered a rarity. Occasionally a walnut case with a mouthpiece of milk glass is located. Double-decker telephones with battery cabinets on the backboards are considered good finds. If you live in the Middle West, you might watch for North Electric Company telephones or Sears Roebuck Company telephones. European telephones are also considered valuable finds in this field.

Almost anything to do with pioneering attempts at communication is today a collectors' item—even items that were made only a short time ago. It has only been a few years since television sets began flooding the market and almost every home in America gave space to this newest item in the entertainment field, yet already some of the early TV sets are considered rare and collectible.

Those models of which only a few sets were made; experimental sets; or sets noted for their size, such as the old three-inch-sets; are collectors' items even today. Who knows what their value will be ten years from now? There were many experimental television sets made, like the eighteen United States Television Projection large-screen sets made in 1947. Certainly there must be many other rare and unique experimental models in existence, which, if they do not fetch a high price today, will do so at some time in the future.

Any radio set that dates back to before 1922 is considered rare and valuable, yet here again the price a collector would pay would depend on how badly he wanted it for his collection. Some types of old radio sets are still rather easy to find in attics, second-hand stores, etc., and it would be wise for the reader to keep an eye out for them. Such sets would include the Crosley and the Radiola. Of the latter, the Model III and III-A are the ones to watch for especially, since these would be the easiest to find. Scarcer items such as the Model I would, of course, have more value.

According to one radio hobbyist, any manufactured radio set (that is, one made by a company and not by an amateur) that uses the UV199, UX199, WD11 and WD12 tubes is now a collectors' item. These sets used dry battery cells to power the filaments. Any old manufactured crystal set using Galena crystal and cat's whisker should also have value.

Western Electric and Marconi sets, some of them dating back to 1910, are rare items. The Phantom Radio Receptor, the Grebe model radio, and the old Atwater Kent Breadboard are considered rare items, the latter being worth from fifteen to twenty dollars. Home-made or amateur-made radio sets, however, have very little value.

Scarcity in itself is not always the criterion in determining the value of old radio sets, since often the collectors only want items that remind them of their youth, or that bring back memories of their work: a former ship's radio operator might want items only in this line, and so on.

Some collectors even want old radio magazines. A copy of *QST* Magazine, which radio hobbyists will recognize as a trade journal, can be worth as much as fifty dollars, if it is the right issue and in good condition.

Phonograph records, sheet music, photographs, newspaper clippings, etc., all have value if they concern famous personalities of the past—or even of the present. Be sure to watch for items concerning the following persons:

> Jack Benny
> Russ Colombo
> Bing Crosby
> Xavier Cugat
> Jimmy Durante
> Bob Hope
> Al Jolson
> Jeanette MacDonald
> Tex Ritter

Private recordings by any of the famous stars of stage, screen or radio are valued by collectors. Old cylinder phonographs are still easy to find and fairly easy to sell to the collectors. Even old instruction books and catalogs for the cylinder phonographs are worth something today.

The *original* Edison styluses are getting rarer and rarer, yet one dealer in the West recently managed to locate a supply of these original styluses that had been stored for many years.

The horns, elbows, even the tubing (connecting horn to reproducer), or any other parts of the old Edison phonographs should not be thrown away. They would have a minimal value, but collectors do want them, sometimes quite badly, if they have one of the old phonographs that has parts missing.

Any really old record is also worth checking, including those of the fabulous Enrico Caruso. These would have to be the originals, of course! Very old and/or rare records of the following types are wanted:

Columbia
Edison
Fonotipia
French Decca
International Zonophone Company
Odéon
Pathé Sapphire Bell
Victor, red seal

Also any kind of very early dance records, that is, pre-1930, are wanted.

Artists in the early recording field whose works are of especial interest are usually those who are the best remembered. For example:

George M. Cohan
Grace Moore
Mary Garden
Al Jolson
Harry Lauder
John McCormack
Nellie Melba

This does not mean that any record made by any of these persons would have value. One of their records *might* have value, if it were old enough and in good enough condition and if it were a missing item on some collector's list. They are all worth checking out.

Even old catalogs issued by the various record companies can be worth ten or eleven dollars. An Edison manual of instructions on how to assemble and set up the attachments for the Edison phonographs has a value of a couple of dollars.

Also, any kind of material on the early motion-picture industry is desirable, and this includes anything from old film magazines to photographs and recordings and other items. Old movie projectors, old movie cameras, film props, etc., are all collectors' items. As a matter of fact, anything connected with the early days of movie-making is desired. This was an incredible era in our entertainment history, a day that will never return and that should be remembered.

Writings, clippings, broadsides, or programs of plays or musicals in the theatre of the past can have value today. Anything connected with the lives of the old stage actors is worth watching for: their diaries, letters, and even clippings concerning them.

Scrapbooks concerned with the stars of the American theatre from the era of Julia Marlowe, the Barrymores, and other American greats, together with items concerning foreign stars like Sarah Bernhardt, can have value if they are complete enough. One such set of scrapbooks was recently added to the theatre collection of the State University at Columbus, Ohio. This series of thirty-four scrapbooks included approximately twenty-five thousand clippings, as well as photographs, theatre programs and various other items dealing with the theatre and its stars of yesteryear.

Watch for old theatre programs and old theatre posters from the late 1800's featuring such names as Edwin Booth. Also, old stage props might have some value, or the costumes of the past.

Programs and mementoes of the old minstrel shows should be watched for—and do not forget vaudeville! Mementoes of the days of vaudeville can become the focal point of a collection.

Burlesque, too, has a place in the various collections. Remember that from burlesque came some of our greatest Broadway talents!

Anything is possible, both in the world of entertainment and in that of the treasure hunter!

XXXIV

THE BLACK VIRGINS OF KAZAN

The Miracle Icons of Russia

RUSSIAN Christians have venerated an icon called the Black Virgin of Kazan for centuries. Because of this veneration, many hundreds of copies of the Black Virgin have been made.

In 1963 a stolen copy of the icon was discovered in San Francisco, Calif. An old man walked into an antique shop and sold a copy of the Black Virgin to the dealer for twenty dollars. Later the dealer saw a photograph of the icon in a local newspaper and knew that he had purchased one of the fabled Black Virgins for a mere twenty dollars. Naturally he then called the police.

The dealer, believing all the gems in the icon to be imitations, had estimated that it was worth up to three hundred dollars, whereas the actual value was closer to fifteen thousand dollars—this despite the fact that the larger emeralds had been removed and sold separately in the 1930's. With the original emeralds the icon—and remember, it was only a copy—would have been worth seventy thousand dollars.

At the time of the theft, the icon was the property of Dr. Lester A. Luz. The Luz icon has a silver enamel and gold *rizza*, or mask, covered with jewels. Designed by Fabergé, it had formerly belonged to the Grand Duke Dmitri Pavlosich and is a fine example of Russian religious art. But, again, it is not a miracle icon, but a copy—and it is only one of hundreds of copies.

The original icon is so special that it is called the miracle icon of Russia. Centuries ago, in a monastery at Kazan, 600 miles from Moscow, there was a small painting on wood of Mary, the Mother of God. Believed to have been painted around 1400, this was the original Black Virgin of Kazan. The legend surrounding it tells of its having been in existence at an even earlier time. In 1209 barbarians from Mongolia swept over the land in hordes, burying everything ahead of them in a bath of blood. At Kazan the people waited, prepared to fight, yet knowing that they could not survive the onslaught of the invaders.

When they saw that their defeat was imminent, they buried the Black Virgin of Kazan in the monastery walls. When the invasion was over, Kazan was a dead place, with no man, woman, or child left alive to tell of the secret hidden in the walls.

Time passed, and new people settled in Kazan and made a new life. Searches were made for the painting, but for almost two and a half centuries the searches were in vain. Then, in 1450, a young girl, so the legend goes, saw golden light surrounding a vision of a face near a certain spot in the ruins of the monastery walls.

The young girl pointed out the spot, and men started digging into the ancient walls. Soon a bundle of rags was laid to view by the picks of the workmen. When the rags were taken apart, the painting of the Virgin was revealed, complete and undamaged. At that moment, the legend continues, the blind of the city regained their sight.

In the latter part of the sixteenth century, invaders swept toward Kazan, and this time the people wavered. Yet the sight of the sacred icon held high in the hands of a priest before the troops brought forth fresh courage and brought victory to the people.

In 1579, a special monastery was built in Kazan to house the icon. In 1612, when invaders, this time from Poland, invaded Russia, the sight of the Black Virgin, which was being brought by forced march from Kazan to Moscow, inspired the people with such courage that the Poles were driven back.

Finally the Great Kazan Cathedral was built in Moscow to house the painting, and in 1630 the original icon was placed in the Cathedral. It is said that the presence of the icon, hidden under the shirt of a Russian marshal, was the real cause of Napoleon's retreat from

Moscow—that famous retreat that eventually set in motion forces that led to Elba and St. Helena.

The Black Virgin of Kazan is a part of Russian history and known all over the world. In the 1870's, the Black Virgin of Kazan was so well known in America that *Harper's Magazine* made special note of it, giving the Cathedral of Kazan in Moscow as its resting place.

But by this time, the Black Virgin was no longer simply a painting, plain yet miraculous. It had become legendary as one of the most beautiful, bejeweled *objets d'art* in the world. The original Black Virgin was showered with gifts by the grateful people she had healed and who venerated her, and these gifts took the form of precious stones. There was such an abundance of gems that the painting had to be partially covered with a mask, leaving only the faces of the Virgin and Child exposed to sight. The mask, or *rizza*, was set with the jewels.

This golden *rizza* was first placed on the icon in about 1600. The *rizza* holds over a thousand gems, including a rare cinnamon diamond, various other diamonds, pearls, rubies, and sapphires. Above this is a halo of emeralds, which are said to be the emeralds that came from Cleopatra's tomb.

One estimate of the value of the Black Virgin is five hundred thousand dollars; another estimate I have seen places the value at three hundred and fifty thousand dollars. A fabulous estimate for a fabulous icon! But then, this is the original of all the Black Virgins. In addition to all the copies, including the Luz copy, there were actually three main or miracle Black Virgins of Kazan.

The two miracle copies of the icon were made in the early 1600's. After the original was taken to Moscow, the village of Kazan wanted an icon, so a copy was made in 1612 and sent back to the village. This is the second main Black Virgin. This copy was destroyed by thieves, who removed the gems in 1904.

Some time after 1612, a second copy was made for St. Petersburg. This is the third main or miracle Black Virgin. During the reign of Peter the Great it was placed in the Cathedral in St. Petersburg. But it was stolen, the jewels pried out, and the icon itself destroyed by fire.

The original Black Virgin is now in the United States. It is the same one that was taken to Moscow in 1612, and that rested in the Kremlin from 1630 until 1917. Following the Revolution in Russia, the Moscow Kazan was taken from the Cathedral and sold by the Communists, who probably sold the icon without knowing that the one they sold was the original.

Not too long ago, in a special television program showing scenes of Moscow, there was shown a Black Virgin. Yet reliable sources state that this Black Virgin was probably painted in either the late 1800's or early 1900's. It had been painted with varnish to give it an appearance of age. The original icon, which is now in the United States, is painted in tempera, sour rye beer having been used in the emulsion. Sour rye beer has not been used in this way since approximately the thirteenth century.

The original icon is now owned by Anna Mitchell-Hedges, Farley Castle, England. At the moment, the Russian Orthodox Greek Church of America is trying to raise money so that the icon may be purchased and re-enshrined at a special Shrine of Our Lady of Kazan, which will be built in San Francisco.

Photographs of the Black Virgin are being sold to help raise funds, and checks and contributions should be mailed to the Fund for Our Lady of Kazan Shrine, 2040 Anza Street, San Francisco 18, Calif.

But what about the hundreds of other Black Virgins? There were so many of them made. Not too long ago, four different Black Virgins were on display in New York City, and all of them were copies of the miracle Virgins.

We know where these are and we know where the Luz Black Virgin is, but there are many, many of these icons waiting to be found, if the treasure hunter knows what he is looking for!

XXXV

CANDLESTICK ROCK IS MISSING

Mementoes of Sports and Games

CANDLESTICK Park in San Francisco has become almost a national institution, but did you know that the rock for which the park was named is missing?

According to the story, there was a rock shaped like a candlestick—and this is why Candlestick Park was named as it was. But Candlestick Rock has disappeared.

It is said that even the photographs of the rock have disappeared, though whether this is true or not, I do not know. In the 1890's, the United States government surveyed the area and specifically mentioned the rock, so that we know that it actually did exist.

The Chamber of Commerce in San Francisco has been completely unsuccessful in its attempts to find out either what happened to the rock or its present location. One theory is that the rock itself was ground up in the cement used in preparing the park for public use.

Whatever happened to it, it is a missing part of baseball Americana —and baseball Americana of all kinds is truly as much a part of the collectors' field as antique rockers or Colonial cooking pots.

Watch especially for older memorabilia of the St. Louis Browns (presently called the Baltimore Orioles). These items can have comparatively great value today, since very little printed publicity was ever issued about them. The daily game score card was about the only thing ever issued.

J. J. Sullivan, writer, collector of sports memorabilia, and one of America's finest experts on antique sports, has managed to collect only twelve St. Louis score cards despite the fact that over four hundred were issued. For most of my material on sports, I am most deeply indebted to Mr. Sullivan.

When Milwaukee replaced Boston in the National League, collectors immediately began to vie for both Boston and Milwaukee memorabilia. As a matter of fact, the memorabilia of any *former* team of the National League is desired.

Recent baseball memorabilia does not have too much value and it is easy to find. It is the older items which the collectors mostly desire. Things like baseball cards with photos of the players on them are becoming of greater value every day, depending on their age and rarity. Also, watch for older items belonging to the Brooklyn Dodgers, the New York Giants (now San Francisco Giants) and Connie Mack's Athletics.

Watch for these baseball memorabilia:

> gum cards
> jewelry
> pennants
> picture sets
> schedule cards
> score cards
> ticket information leaflets
> ticket stubs
> yearbooks

If you saw an inflated ox bladder, would you recognize it as a football? Maybe not, but that's what it might be. As early as the middle sixteen hundreds, this kind of ball was used in a game between Bostonians and neighboring Indians.

Watch for old souvenir football programs. These come in all sizes, types of print and value. And football score cards are also collectors' items.

Don't forget golfing items. All golfing memorabilia, of course, must be either rare or old or unusual and sometimes all three. The early 1900's in America produced both golf clubs and golf balls, but these are not worth very much; Scottish golf balls are rare, however, and

Scottish feathery balls are in demand.

European golf books which specifically refer to golfing rules in Scotland may sometimes have great value. There are some very famous older golfing prints, and there are also paintings on golf by such American artists as Grant and Richards.

Old magazines sometimes have old golfing prints in them. Magazines that have golfing themes on the covers are especially desired. Golf trophies, however, are not worth much, nor are regular cards with neither romantic nor comic representations of the game of golf. Romantic and funny or comic golfing postcards can have a much greater value, however, than, say, hatpins with a golfing theme. It all depends, probably, upon rarity. Golfing ashtrays, for example, are not rare at all.

Remember, however, that it would be a good idea to watch for:

> clubs
> cocktail shakers
> curios
> drinking cups
> golf balls
> golf steins
> platters
> prints
> Wedgwood plates, vases, etc.

Games of all kinds are worth watching for. Also, watch for old puzzles. Most puzzles date from the 1910's and 1920's although there are puzzles which were made before 1900, and these older puzzles are mostly wooden or made of wire. There are advertising puzzles from the 1890's.

Some of the old wooden puzzles are hand carved. There are also old puzzles made of tile and glass that are wanted by the collectors. Home-made puzzles, also. Willis R. Bush, a New York puzzle collector, seems to feel that the pre-1900 wire puzzles are the hardest to solve. Easy to find in the puzzle field would be old block puzzles, so named because they resemble children's play blocks.

The modern manufacturers are still making puzzles, some of them identical to the older, antique puzzles, but the workmanship by comparison suffers badly. The modern puzzles cannot stand up to comparison with the antique puzzles—at least according to the collectors of antique puzzles.

Puzzles, games and sports memorabilia all should be old, preferably found in quantity, rare and in as good condition as possible. The scope of this field is unbelievable.

Watch for:

> books on sports
> boxing gloves
> dumbbells
> ice skates
> Indian clubs
> punching bags
> sleds
> sports magazines
> tennis balls
> tennis rackets
> wooden decoys

XXXVI

Sunken and Buried Treasure

Treasure in the Earth and under the Sea

THERE is a two-hundred-thousand-dollar car at the bottom of the ocean, probably the strangest of all the sunken treasure in the sea.

On July 25, 1956, on a foggy night on the Atlantic Ocean, the Italian liner *Andrea Doria* was rammed by a Swedish-American Line ship, the *Stockholm*. In the collision, fifty people died, but thousands were saved in rescue operations. What they could not save was the *Andrea Doria* herself and the cargo she carried.

Attempts to salvage the *Andrea Doria* have been made. She still lies at the bottom of the sea, but if and when she is raised, she will be worth millions.

On that ship when she went down was the Chrysler "idea car" on which two hundred thousand dollars had been spent. The car was being shipped from Italy, and it would have been the first time that the car had been shown to the public. Unless the *Andrea Doria* can be raised, the car can be considered a complete loss.

Designed by the Chrysler Corporation Engineering Division, the car was built by Ghia of Turin, in complete secrecy. Chrysler had spent a year designing the car and another year and three months having it built. They called it the "Norseman."

Brand-new ideas had gone into the Norseman:

(1) The only interruption in the glass around the passenger compartment was two steel arches in the rear.

(2) There were no posts or pillars supporting the roof.

(3) There was a glass panel in the roof of the car that could be opened and closed.

The engine in this Chrysler dream car was a special, advanced Chrysler engine. The trunk lid, the door handles, and the automatic headlights were all concealed. Truly an American dream car.

GOLD, as the saying goes, is all round you—in the form of sunken treasure, buried treasure, lost mines and ships sunk at sea.

Less than ten miles from Murphy, Ore., there is a cave, in which, if you can find it, is the Lost Badger Mine.

A Mormon with five feuding wives found what he described as a whole mountain of gold somewhere between Salt Lake City, Utah and Carson City, Nev. Between hostile Indians and his five angry wives, he kept going and never found the mountain of gold again. This one is called the Lost Bonanza Mine.

A man called Pegleg Smith once walked from Yuma to San Diego. Exhausted and ill, he was taken to the hospital where attendants found over a thousand dollars worth of gold in his pockets. Questions were put to him. Once during the long trek, he told them, he had spotted two peaks. He had climbed one of the peaks to get a better idea of where he was, and that was how he found the gold. Pegleg died, and the spot where he found his gold has never been relocated. But the story of his mine, the Lost Pegleg, continues as one of the most famous of the lost mine legends.

Somewhere in the High Sierras in California, three prospectors found a seam of cement rock studded with gold. They hid their find, brought samples out to be assayed and headed back for civilization. A fight broke out over the ultimate possession of the rich mine, and only one man made it to civilization, although he was dying.

Before he died he gave a map and his samples to one Gid Whiteman. Whiteman disappeared into the mountains and was never seen again. There were rumors about him, alleged sightings of him, but this was only wishful thinking on the part of those who hoped he would turn up with the secret of the Lost Cement Mine, for this is the name that men gave to the cement rock studded with gold.

Then a find was made high in the Sierras. It was dubbed the Mammoth Mine, and many people said it was really the Lost Cement Mine. Others claim the Lost Cement Mine is still lost. No one really knows. The cement rock studded with gold may still be hidden high in the Sierras, waiting for someone to find it.

Then there is the treasure of Neahkahne Mountain in Oregon, somewhere close to Highway 101. In the early 1600's, the crew of a Spanish ship, wrecked off the Oregon coast, salvaged what treasure they could and buried it on Neahkahne Mountain. According to the Seaside, Ore., Chamber of Commerce, there have been many people who have looked for the Treasure of Neahkahne, but so far no one has been successful in locating it.

The treasures of the Incas, the Mayans and the Aztecs bring dreams of treasure to everyone. Edward Thompson found a sacrificial well of the ancient Mayans at Chichen Itza and brought out of that well reptiles and monkeys of gold, golden candlesticks and golden bells, golden masks and golden earrings: a veritable fortune. But with the golden objects he brought out, he also located the skeletons of those who were sacrificed. Thompson did not get all the items up from the well at Chichen Itza, however. It is estimated that, although he did take out several million dollars' worth of treasure, there is still gold in Chichen Itza. And this is only one sacrificial well. There are others in Mexico.

Another item that is representative of the amount of treasure left in the lands to the south of us is a twelve-ton chain of golden links, which is only a small part of a fifty-million-dollar cache of Indian treasure hidden somewhere in Peru—or at least this is how the legend goes.

Gold and silver treasure is literally all around you—buried pirate loot, lost mines, buried war loot and sunken ships. You may have to travel a few miles to your location, but, with luck, a proper background of research and the proper equipment, you could become a millionaire!

Over seventy million dollars' worth of pirate treasure went down in the ocean near Pensacola, Fla., not more than forty miles from land. A pirate by the curious name of Billy Bowlegs Rogers supposedly buried treasure somewhere along the Florida coast. A treasure worth five million dollars was lost when the *Merida* sank near Cape Charles, Va.

The *Santa Margarita* was wrecked in a sudden hurricane somewhere in the neighborhood of Palm Beach, Fla. The ship went down, carrying about a million dollars with it to the bottom. Not too long ago, a diver went down in those waters to do some repair work on a cable and found the *Santa Margarita.* He had to leave the area, however, and it was two years before he could return with the proper equipment to salvage the treasure. But, before he could begin work, a hurricane wrecked his boat, and several of the crew were killed. The diver himself was saved and later he tried again, but he could never relocate the wreck of the *Santa Margarita.*

A bootlegger working off the coast of Florida was luckier. After spotting a sunken ship, he was able to bring up thousands of dollars' worth of coins. And once, off the coast of Colombo, Ceylon, a man and two boys took a day off from filming an underwater movie. Their day off was well spent. They went exploring under water for fun and found quantities of silver, two cannons, some copper bars and lead shot.

In the course of a story of mutiny and murder, the crewmen of the *Don Carlos* buried millions of dollars' worth of Spanish coins on the Isle of Pines in the West Indies. I have heard that a map showing the location of this treasure is extant, but no one has yet found the gold. This map may really be in existence; the point is that often such maps, even when authentic, are very difficult to decipher.

Once a man, using an authentic treasure map, found the two cannons that had been drawn on the map, then he spent years trying to empty a lagoon at which the cannons had pointed. After his death, another man found the treasure inside the cannons themselves.

Sometimes sunken treasure is closer to home than we might expect it to be. The *Dean Richmond* went down in Lake Erie, carrying, in addition to other cargo, one hundred and forty-one thousand dollars. The *Clarion,* with over a hundred thousand dollars in bullion, sank in Lake Erie in the early 1900's. And these are only two among thousands of ships wrecked in the Great Lakes. The *Lexington,* with gold and silver bullion aboard, lies at the bottom of New York City's East River.

If you want to go after buried or sunken treasure, however, you must know what you're doing! Finding buried or sunken treasure is only for those with the heart and brains for adventure. Those who set out to find this kind of treasure equipped with nothing but a handful of dreams and a minimum of prior study are doomed to failure before they start.

The seeker of sunken or buried treasure must do all the research he can before starting out. Read all the existing literature on the particular treasure you wish to find. Try to sort out, when possible, the legends from the facts concerning your treasure, keeping in mind that stories tend to grow and become more fantastic as they are told and retold over the years.

Write to appropriate sources for further information—treasure experts; the chamber of commerce of the region where the the treasure is located; the state information service in the state capital, for information on treasure laws in that state; and the federal government, asking for information on the federal treasure laws. (Both state and federal treasure laws apply to sunken as well as to buried treasure.)

And after you have found your treasure, assuming that you are allowed to keep it under existing treasure laws, then it's time to remember the income-tax man!

My advice to the reader, however, is that he concentrate on those treasures that can be found closer to home—in the form of rare books, old coins, art objects, etc. These items could be found in your attic, your basement, the neighborhood second-hand stores or even in the city dump. And conducting this kind of search is a lot less expensive than going on a jaunt to some far-off place for lost treasure.

And, above all, keep your wits about you. Don't be like the woman who found some rocks that tested very high in uranium content—and then couldn't remember where she'd found them!

BIBLIOGRAPHY

ABBOTT, JOHN C. S. *Italy*. New York: Co-Operative Publishing Co., 1882. *States*. New York: Harper and Brothers, 1931.

ADAMS, EPHRAIM DOUGLASS, AND ALMACK, JOHN C. *A History of the United States*. New York: Harper and Brothers, 1931.

AGENCY OF THE BRITISH GOVERNMENT. "The Crown Jewels" (brochure), San Francisco, Calif.: 1952.

ARRINGTON, JOSEPH EARL. "John Banvard's Moving Panorama of the Mississippi, Missouri and Ohio Rivers," *Filson Club Quarterly* (July, 1958).

ATWOOD, ALBERT W. "Stately Homes of Old Virginia," *National Geographic Magazine* (June, 1953).

BAERWALD, MARCUS. *The Story of Jewelry*. London: Abelard-Schuman, Ltd., 1960.

BAKAL, CARL. "Campaign Pushbuttons," *True Magazine* (October, 1960).

BALZELL, W. J. *A Complete History of Music, for Schools and Private Reading*. Philadelphia: Theodore Presser Co., 1905.

BANKS, GORDON T. "The Auction Market" (in Autograph column conducted by K. V. Hostick), *Hobbies Magazine* (May, 1962).

BARBET, P·ERRE. *A Doctor at Calvary, the Passion of Our Lord Jesus Christ as Described by a Surgeon*. New York: P. J. Kenedy and Sons, 1950.

BARKER, VIRGIL. *American Painting*. New York: The Macmillan Co., 1950.

BARTON, FRANCIS. "Holy Shroud of Turin," *Fate Magazine* (August, 1954).

BAUM, A. S. "A 'Masonic' Hobby," *The Beacon* (March, 1961).

BENTLEY, JOHN. *Antique Automobiles*, New York: Fawcett Publications, 1952.

BERTHE, ABBÉ EDWARD. *The Life of the Blessed Virgin Mary, with the History of the Devotion to Her*. New York: ——, ——.

BIERCE, AMBROSE. *Can Such Things Be?* New York: Jonathan Cape and Harrison Smith, 1909.

BISHOP, JIM. *The Day Lincoln Was Shot*. New York: Harper and Brothers, 1955.

BORAH, LEO A., AND REVIS, KATHLEEN. "Landmarks of Literary England," *National Geographic Magazine* (September, 1955).

BREDIUS, A. *The Paintings of Rembrandt*. Vienna: Phaidon Verlag, 1936.

BURGESS, FRED W. *Antique Jewelry and Trinkets*. New York: Tudor Publishing Co., 1937.

CHAFFIN, LORAH B. *Sons of the West.* Caldwell, Ida.: Caxton Printers, Ltd., 1941.

CHESNEY, W. D. "There Was a Jesus of Nazareth," *Fate Magazine* (August, 1954).

CHURCH OF JESUS CHRIST OF LATTER DAY SAINTS. *Book of Mormon.* Salt Lake City, Utah.

———. *Doctrines and Covenants of the Church of Jesus Christ of Latter Day Saints.* Salt Lake City, Utah: 1952.

CLARKE, ARTHUR C. "Their Skin Diving Paid Off," *This Week Magazine* (New York) (April, 1962).

CLYMER, FLOYD. "1909-1959, Fifty Years of Progress," *The Man's Magazine* (November, 1958).

COLE, WILLIAM D. "Treasure Below," *Argosy Magazine* (August, 1958).

COLLIER, W. D. "The Scottish Regalia, anciently styled the Honours of Scotland" (brochure) (July, 1951).

COOKSON, JOHN. *Before the African Storm.* New York: Bobbs-Merrill Co., 1954.

CRAVEN, THOMAS. *The Rainbow Book of Art.* New York: World Publishing Co., 1956.

DAVENPORT, HENRY. *Grandest Century in the World's History.* Kansas City, Mo.: Northrup Topeka Book Co., 1900.

DAWSON, GILES. "What Happened to Shakespeare's Manuscripts?", *Texas Quarterly* (Autumn, 1961).

DREPPERD, CARL W. *American Arts and Artists.* Springfield, Mass.: Pond-Eckberg Co., 1962.

———, *Pioneer America, Its First Three Centuries.* New York: Doubleday and Co., 1949.

———. *Primer of American Antiques.* New York: Doubleday Doran and Co., 1944.

EISENSCHIML, OTTO. *In the Shadow of Lincoln's Death.* New York: Wilfred Funk, Inc., 1940.

EMERSON, EDWIN, JR. *A History of the Nineteenth Century Year by Year.* New York: P. F. Collier and Son, 1900.

ENGEL, LOUIS. *How To Buy Stocks.* Boston: Little, Brown and Co., 1953.

EPSTEIN, RALPH. *Making Money in Today's Market.* New York: Smith, Keynes and Marshall, 1959.

FAWCETT, CLARA B. "Kate Greenaway's Dolls," *Hobbies Magazine* (November, 1961).

———. "Swiss Mechanical Dolls," *Hobbies Magazine* (September, 1961).

FERTIG, LAWRENCE. "The Flow of Gold," *American Legion Magazine* (May, 1962).

FISHER, ALLAN C. "Eastman of Rochester: Photographic Pioneer," *National Geographic Magazine* (September, 1954).

FLITCH, J. E. C. *The National Gallery.* Boston: Small, Maynard and Co., 1912.

FLOWER, ENOLA. *A Child's History of California.* ———: California State Department of Education, 1949.

FOSHAG, W. F. "Exploring the World of Gems," *National Geographic Magazine* (December, 1950).

FOSTER, CONSTANCE J. *The Story of Money*. New York: Medill McBride and Co., 1950.

FRANKENSTEIN, ALFRED. "Each Lincolnized Portrait Was Itself a Copy," *San Francisco Sunday Chronicle* (San Francisco, Calif.) (February, 1962).

———. "101 American Primitive Paintings," *San Francisco Sunday Chronicle* (San Francisco, Calif. (August, 1962).

FRENCH, CHARLES. "Numismatics," *Hobbies Magazine* (August, 1962).

GAINES, EDITH. "Woman's Day Dictionary of Furniture," *Woman's Day Magazine* (August, 1960).

GARRICK, ALICE VAN LEER. *Collector's Luck*. Boston: Atlantic Monthly Press, 1919.

GRAY, RALPH. "Vacation Tour through Lincoln Land," *National Geographic Magazine* (February, 1952).

GREEN, JOHN RICHARD. *England*. New York: Co-Operative Publication Society, ———.

GUIZOT, M. AND DE WITT, MME. GUIZOT. *France*. New York Co-Operative Publication Society, ———.

HAWTHORNE, JULIAN. *United States*. New York: Peter Fenelon Galleries, 1898.

HENRY, OMER. "Is There a Fortune Waiting for You?", *Family Weekly* (May, 1959).

HERST, HERMAN, JR. *Fun and Profit in Stamp Collecting*. New York: Duell, Sloan and Pearce, 1962.

———. "How To Sell Your United States Stamps" (brochure) (Shrub Oak, N.Y.).

HESTON, JUDY. "Memorabilia of Old Campaigns," *San Francisco Chronicle* (San Francisco, Calif.) (March, 1962).

HICKS, CLIFFORD B. (ed.) "Detroit. Where Are Those Old Time 'Touches'?", *Popular Mechanics* (March, 1962).

HUGHES, RUPERT. *The Biographical Dictionary of Musicians*. New York: Blue Ribbon Books, Inc., 1940.

JENSEN, OLIVER. "Don't Boil the Calliope Player or Good News for Music Lovers," *American Heritage Magazine* (August, 1960).

——— (ed.) "Prodigious Panorama," *American Heritage Magazine* (December, 1960).

KAMM, MINNIE WATSON. *A Third Two Hundred Pattern Glass Pitchers*. New York: Century House, 1943.

KEELEY, JOSEPH C. "Those Old Time Circus Days," *American Legion Magazine* (May, 1962).

KEMP, P. K., AND LLOYD, CHRISTOPHER. *Brethren of the Coast, Buccaneers of the South Seas*. New York: St. Martin's Press, 1960.

KLEIN, JERRY. "Can They Raise the Andrea Doria?", *Family Weekly* (August 3, 1958).

KNOP, FRED. "Six Hundred Brands Are Just a Start for Cattleman Hobbyist," *Cutter Standard* (Berkeley, Calif.) (fall, 1960).

KORNITZER, LOUIS. *The Gem Trader*. New York: Sheridan House, 1939.

KREH, WILLIAM. "Science Overseas," *Popular Mechanics* (June, 1962).

LEE, RUTH WEBB. *Victorian Glass, Specialties of the Nineteenth Century*. Framingham Centre, Mass.: published by the author, 1944.

LEY, WILLY. "Space Prospectors," *Space World* (1961).

LIEBER, LESLIE. "Mystery of Venus's Arms," *This Week Magazine* (New York) (March, 1962).

LOREN, STEFAN. "Solved: The Great Lincoln Portrait Mystery," *This Week Magazine* (New York) (February, 1962).

LUPTON, F. M. *Family Cyclopedia of Useful Knowledge*. New York: John S. Dorn, 1889.

LYON, PETER. "The Wild Wild West," *American Heritage Magazine* (August, 1960).

MALICK. "Malick's Fossils" (brochure), (Baltimore, Md.) (fall, 1962).

MARTIN, GORDON. "The Harrah Automobile Collection," *San Francisco Sunday Chronicle* (San Francisco, Calif.) (July, 1962).

MCCLINTON, KATHERINE MORRISON. *Antique Collecting*. New York: Fawcett Publications, Inc., 1952.

MCCRACKEN, HAROLD. *The Charles M. Russell Book, the Life and Work of the Cowboy Artist*. New York: Doubleday and Co., 1957.

MENZEL, WOLFGANG. *Germany*. New York: Co-Operative Publication Society, ———.

MOORE, N. HUDSON. *The Old Furniture Book With A Sketch of Past Days and Ways*. New York: Frederick A. Stokes Co., 1903.

NESM TH, ROBERT I. "Black Hearts and Bibliography," *Eye to Eye: Bulletin of the Graphic History Society of America* (September, 1954).

———. "Collecting a Private Library," *Avocations* (May, 1938).

NEWMAN, JULIA SWEET. "Autograph Letters," "American Historical Material" (brochures) (Battle Creek, Mich.).

NORDUE, HOWARD W. "Apothecariana, the Mortar and Pestle," *Hobbies Magazine* (May, 1961).

ORMSBEE, THOMAS HAMILTON. *The Story of American Furniture*. New York: The Macmillan Co., 1934.

OWEN, PAT. "Bing and Grondahl Christmas Plates," *Hobbies Magazine* (December, 1961).

PARKE BERNET GALLERIES. "English Furniture and Decorations," *Public Auction Catalog*. New York: 1961.

PETERS, HARRY T. *Currier and Ives, Printmakers to the American People*. New York: Doubleday and Co., 1942.

PETERSON, ARTHUR G. *Salt and Pepper Shakers*. Washington, D.C.: Washington College Press, ——.

PORGES, IRWIN. "Unburied Treasure," *Coronet Magazine* (1957).

PRATT, FLETCHER. *Civil War in Pictures*. New York: Garden City Books, 1955.

PULNAM, JOHN. *The Largest Picture Ever Executed by Man*. Boston: [Printer No. 81], 1847.

PUTNAM, GEORGE PALMER. *Putnam's Handbook of Universal History*. New York: G. P. Putnam's Sons, 1907.

RALPH, EDWARD. *The Early Victorian Period, 1830-1860*. New York: Reynal and Co., 1958.

REEDER, PEARL ANN (ed.) "America Goes to the Polls," *Hobbies Magazine* (November, 1960).

——. "Americana Page," *ibid.* (July, 1961).

——. "Chicago Tribune Brings $70 at Auction," *ibid.* (July, 1962).

——. "Hallowe'en Witch Figures," *ibid.* (November, 1961).

——. "Medicine Exhibit," *ibid.* (November, 1961).

——. "Rare Theatre Collection Goes to Ohio Museum," *ibid.* (April, 1962).

REINFELD, FRED. *A Treasury of American Coins*. Garden City, N.Y.: Hanover House, 1961.

RIESEBERG, HARRY. "Harry Rieseberg's Treasure Chest," *Cavalier Magazine* (September, 1959).

RIGBY, DOUGLAS AND ELIZABETH. *Lock, Stock and Barrel: A Story of Collecting*. Philadelphia: J. B. Lippincott Co., 1944.

RIPLEY. *Ripley's Believe It or Not*. New York: Pocket Books, Inc., 1958.

ROGERS, FRED B. "Candlestick's Mystery," *San Francisco Chronicle* (San Francisco, Calif.) (April, 1962).

ROSCOE, THEODORE, AND FREEMAN, FRED. *Picture History of the United States Navy*. New York: Charles Scribner's Sons, 1956.

SANDOZ, CECILE. "Paris Exclusive: An Elaborate City of Art, Antiques," *San Francisco Sunday Chronicle* (San Francisco, Calif.) (June, 1962).

SCHLEGEL, DOROTHY M. *Gem Stones of the United States*. Washington, D.C.: Government Printing Office, 1957.

SCHWARZ, NORMAN. "Gamble for the Sun God's Gold," *True Magazine* (November, 1958).

SHERMAN, CARL. "Who Owns the Skull of Mkwawa Rules Africa," *Bluebook* (July, 1962).

SIMPSON, WILL AM R. AND FLORENCE K. *Hockshop*. New York: Random House, 1954.

SMEDBERG, W. R., III. *United States Naval Academy Catalog of Information*. Annapolis, Md.: U.S. Naval Academy, 1962.

SMITH, G. F. HERBERT. *Gem Stones and Their Distinctive Characters*. London: Methuen and Co., 1912.

SMITH, MAURICE. *A Short History of Dentistry*. New York: Roy Publishers, 1958.

SMITHSONIAN INSTITUTION. *Annual Report of the Board of Regents of the Smithsonian Institution*. Washington, D.C.: Government Printing Office, 1906.

SOUCHAL, GENEVIEVE. *French Eighteenth Century Furniture, Pleasures and Treasures*. New York: G. P. Putnam's Sons, ———.

STIRLING, N. "The $280,000,000 Treasure Hunt," *Argosy* (July, 1956).

SUNNERS, WILLIAM. *How and Where to Find the Facts*. New York: Arco Publishing Co., 1963.

SWITZER, GEORGE S. "The Many Sided Diamond," *National Geographic Magazine* (April, 1958).

THOMPSON, EDWARD. *Last of the Elizabethans*. New Haven: Yale University Press, 1936.

TUNIS, EDWIN. *Wheels, A Pictorial History*. New York: World Publishing Co., 1955.

TURNER, VICTOR. A Fascinating Hobby," *Hobbies Magazine* (January, 1963).

TWINING, LORD. *A History of the Crown Jewels of Europe*. London: B. T. Batsford, 1960.

United States and Canadian Coins, Premium Guide and Check List (brochure), Cincinnati, Ohio, 1960.

WANGLER, LA VAUGHN. "Antique Greeting Cards from the Hallmark Collection" (brochure), Kansas City, Mo.

"Wanted: Personal Documents" (editorial), *Image* (November, 1957).

WARD, DON. *Cowboys and Cattle Country*. In collaboration with the editors of American Heritage. New York: American Heritage Publishing Co., ———.

WARREN, LOUIS A. "Lincoln Lore," *Bulletin of the Lincoln National Life Foundation*, Fort Wayne, Ind., ———.

WEDE, KARL F. " 'Old Salt' Items Are the Spice of Wede's Life," *The Antique Dealer* (April, 1958).

WELLS, H. G. *The Outline of History*. Garden City, N.Y.: Garden City Books, 1961.

WILLIAMS, MAYNARD OWEN. "Pennsylvania Dutch Folk Festival," *National Geographic Magazine* (1952).

WRENCH, SIR EVELYN. "The British Way, Alfred the Great," *National Geographic Magazine* (April, 1949).

WUENSCHEL, EDWARD S. *Self Portrait of Christ, the Holy Shroud of Turin*. Esopus, N.Y.: Holy Shroud Guild, 1954.

YARMON, MORTON. *Early American Antique Furniture*. New York: Fawcett Publications, Inc., 1952.

YEOMAN, R. S., *et al. Handbook of United States Coins*. Racine, Wis.: Whitman Publishing Co., 1954.

YOUNG, BOB. "Mystery of the Lost Cement Mine," *Real West Magazine* (July, 1963).

ZIM, HERBERT S., AND SHAFFER, PAUL R. *Rocks and Minerals: A Guide to Familiar Minerals, Gems, Ores and Rocks*. New York: Golden Press, Inc., 1957.

INDEX

A of Charlemagne, 89
Abcderia, 101
Across the Plains in '64
(Collins), 81
Adams, John, 122
Adams furniture, 142
Adrift in New York (Alger),
115
Adventure (magazine), 119
Adventures of Tom Sawyer
(Twain), 112
Advertisements, 67-70
Lion and Arbuckle Coffee,
68
Old Crow Whiskey, 67-68
Underwood Deviled Ham,
68
Africa, 51-52
"After the Bath" (Degas), 65
Age (Burroughs), 116
Alden, John, 144
Alexander III, 17, 19
Alfred the Great, 54, 162
Alger, Horatio, 114
Ali Pasha, 37
Alice in Wonderland
(Carroll), 112
Allison, 123
Altman, Lawrence, 140
Amati, Nicolò, 46
Amber, 176
Amber balls, 159
Ambergris, 14, 158-159
Amelung glass, 131, 133

Amelung Glass Factory, 133
Andrea Doria (liner), 195
Andrewes, Gerrard, 53
"Antioch Chalice," 71-73
Antoinette, Marie, 8, 9
Apollo, 57
Apostle spoons, 166-167
Apple of Discord, 60
Argosy (magazine), 120
"Aristotle Contemplating the
Bust of Homer"
(Rembrandt), 65
Armstrong, 81
Army Navy Weekly
(magazine), 120
Arnold, Benedict, 28
Artifacts, 67-70
cramp rings, 70
dental equipment, 70
dentures, 70
drugstore items, 69
medical instruments, 69
medical rings, 70
mouse traps, 69
scientific instruments, 69
typewriters, 69
Wall Street items, 69
Associated Firemen's
Insurance Company of
Baltimore, Md., 156
Associated Firemen's
Insurance Company of
Pittsburgh, Pa., 156
Atwater Kent breadboard, 183

Auschwitz, Germany, 8
Australian Andamooks Opal, 179
Autographs, 27-32
  Barnum, Phineas T., 30
  Corey, Martha, 28
  Franklin, Benjamin, 28
  Frietchie, Barbara, 28
  Glenn, John, 27
  Hancock, John, 27
  Lincoln, Abraham, 20
  Lind, Jenny, 30
  Napoleon I, 28
  Shakespeare, William, 7, 29-30
  tips on locating, 31-32
  witches, 99

Baby tenders, 100-101
Bache, Anthony, 37
Back to Stone (Burroughs), 116
Baltimore, Lord, 8
Baltimore Equitable Society, 155-156
Banvard, John, 84-85
Barbed wire,
  patent no. 157124, 80
Barber poles, 128-129
Barnum, Phineas T., 30
Barnum's Museum, 25
Barrett, S. M., 81
Barrymore family, 186
Bastille, key to, 98
Beauharnais, Josèphine de, 88
Bell, John, 182
Bellflower cake plates, 133
Bells, 137-40
  types desired, 140
Ben Barclay's Courage (Alger), 115
Benny, Jack, 184
Benz, Carl, 75
Bergonzi, Carlo, 47

Bernhardt, Sarah, 186
Bibles, 116
Bierce, Ambrose, 95
Big Nose Kate, 79
Billings, William, 50
Billy the Kid, 79
Bishop, Bridget, 99
Bishop, William, 37
Bixby, Mrs., 20-22
Black Christs, 90
Black Death, 90
Black Mask (magazine), 120
Black Virgins, 90, 187-190
Blackberry water pitchers, 133
Blaine, James G., 182
Blue Hope diamond, 148
Bohemian glass, 134
Bolec, Amédée, 75
Book of Mormon, 8
Books
  first editions, 9
  rare and valuable editions, 112-120
  Adventures of Tom Sawyer (Twain), 112
  Alger, Horatio, 114-115
  Alice in Wonderland (Carroll), 112
  The Marvelous Land of Oz (Baum), 114
  Murders in the Rue Morgue (Poe), 112
  A New Wonderland (Baum), 114
  Shakespeare, William, 112, 113
  subjects desired, 118-119
  The Wonderful Wizard of Oz (Baum), 113-114
Booth, Edwin, 186
Borgia, Cesare, 63, 64
"Boston Boys and General Gage, The" (print), 123

Boston Journal (newspaper), 29

Boston Transcript (newspaper), 20

Bostonian Society, 22

Boughton, George H., 64

Bowie, James, 81

Bracelets, 162

Brandon, Richard, 98

Brasher, Ephraim, 107

Brasher Doubloon, 107

Brewerton, George D., 81

Brewster furniture, 144

British Guiana stamps, 170-177

British Museum, 130, 161

Brooches, 162

Browning, Elizabeth, 118

Browning, Robert, 118

Bryan, William J., 182

Bulto, 91-92

Burke, Jane, 80

Burns, Robert, 118

Burroughs, Edgar Rice, 115, 118

Burroughs, George, 99

Burrus, M., 171

Bush, Willis R., 193

Butler, Colonel T. P., 35

Butterflies, 9

By Ox Team to California (Porter), 81

Caen, Herb, 9

Cagots, 94

Calamity Jane, 80

California Cut-off Trail, 82

Campaign memorabilia, 180-182

  Brown pens, 180

  Dewey pens, 180

  Lincoln and Hamlin slug, 181

  McKinley pails, 180

  Nixon pens, 180

  types desired, 181-182

  Wilkie-McNary pens, 180

Campaign slogans

  Full Dinner Pail, 180

  God Bless America, 180

  Help Hoover Help Business, 180

  Long Live the President, 181

  Roosevelt and Relief, 180

  Wilkie and Work, 180

Candlestick Rock, 191

Carmi, Avner, 14-15

Carriages, 74-78

Carrier, Martha, 99

Carroll, Lewis, 118

Cars, 74-78

  fire engines, 77

  Harrah's Collection, 76

  L'Obeissante, 75

  Long Island Automobile Museum, 75

  Museum of Science and Industry, 75

  Smithsonian Institute, 76

Caruso, Enrico, 48, 184

Carver furniture, 144

Cass, Lewis, 182

Catcher in the Rye (Salinger), 9

Cello, Bergonzi, 47

Cézanne, Paul, 65, 66

Chambers, Thomas, 85, 86

Charlemagne, 88

Charles I, 98

Charles II, 35

Chessman, Caryl, 95

China, 164-167

  Staffordshire, 13

Chippendale, Thomas, 141

Chisholm Trail, 82

Chisholm Trail, The (Ridings), 81

Christian, King, 17, 34
Chrysler Corporation
    Engineering Division, 195
Church, 75
Cigar-store Indian, 127-128
Cistercian Monks, 90
Citizens' Fire, Marine and
    Life Insurance Company,
    157
City Insurance Company of
    Cincinnati, Ohio, 155
Civil War, 30, 123, 125,
    172-174
Clarion (ship), 198
Clark, William, 10
Clary, Robert de, 41
Clay, Henry, 182
Clay Fire and Marine
    Insurance Company, 156
Cleopatra, 189
"Climbing Over Rocky
    Mountain" (Gilbert and
    Sullivan), 49
Clinton, De Witt, 182
Clocks, 137-140
    Nürenberg Egg watch, 139
    types desired, 139-140
Clothing, 137-140
    corsets, 138
    Dior New Look, 137
    fabrics, 138
    mummy cloths, 138
    Peter Thompson outfit, 138
    types desired, 139
Clyde's Pipe Rack (store), 127
Coaches, 74-78
    Conestoga wagons, 78
    red-flag low, 75-76
Cohan, George M., 185
Coins, 106-108
College of St. Albert the
    Great, 89
Collins, John S., 81
Colombo, Russ, 184

Colossus of Rhodes, 8, 57-58
Columbia (phonograph
    record), 185
Comic books, 117
Commodore, Rollingpin, 117
Conestoga wagons, 78
Confederate stamps, 172-174
*Conservatoire National des
    Arts et Métiers*, 74, 75
"Constitution and the
    Guerrière, The"
    (painting), 86
Copley, John Singleton, 65
Corey, Giles, 99
Corey, Martha, 28
Cosmopolitan (magazine),
    120
Cox, James, 181, 182
Cradles, 100
Crater, Judge, 94
Crater of Diamonds, 146-147
Crawford, William H., 182
Cristallo glass, 131
Crockett, Davy, 117
Croghan (Indian scout), 82
Cromwell, Oliver, 8, 37
Crosby, Bing, 184
Crosley (radio set), 183
Crow, James, 67
Crown Derby china, 166
Crusaders lost treasures,
    109-111
Cugat, Xavier, 184
Cugnot, Nicholas Joseph, 74,
    75
Culpeper family, 8
Currier, Nathaniel, 121-123
Custer, George Armstrong, 80
Cutler, Manasseh, 144
Cuyp family, 64
Cyprian, Saint, 52

Daguerre, Louis Jacques
    Mandé, 124

Daimler, Gottlieb, 75
Dan the Detective (Alger), 115
Dance, Sir Charles, 75
d'Ancre, Marshal, 137
Danton, Georges Jacques, 28
Darktowns (prints), 122
Darnley, Lord, 93
Darwin, Charles, 29
Davis, John W., 181, 182
Dawson, Giles E., 113
De la Roche, 41
Dean Dunham (Alger), 115
Dean Richmond (ship), 198
Death records, 8
Degas, Edgar, 65
Delaware and Lackawanna Railroad, 83
Denmark, lost gems, 34
Deutsches Museum, 75
Dewey, Thomas E., 182
Diamonds, 146-150
Dickens, Charles, 117, 118
Dior, Christian, 137
Directoire period furniture, 143
Documents, 27-32
  auction lists, 31
  Constitution of France, 9
  Johnstown Flood, 30
  jury lists, 29
  Old West, 82
Dodgson, Charles L., *see* Carroll, Lewis
Dolls, 102-103
Don Carlos (ship), 198
Douglas, Stephen A., 182
Duncan Phyfe furniture, 144, 145
Dunnottar Castle, 36
Durante, Jimmy, 184
Duryea, Charles E., 75
Duryea, Frank J., 75, 77

Duyckinck, Evert, 65
d'Zurko, Arpad, 12-13

Earhart, Amelia, 93
Early Cattle Days in Wyoming (Moore), 81
Earp, Wyatt, 79
Eastman, George, 124
Easty, Mary, 99
Edinburgh Castle, 36
Edison, Thomas A., 184
Edison (phonograph record), 185
Edward I, 55
Edward III, 37
Edward VII, 53
Ehrgott, Forbriger and Co., 123
Elizabeth I, Queen, 29
Elizabeth II, Queen, 179
Embroidery, 159-160
Emeralds, 177
Emmanuel III, 14
Empire period furniture, 143
English crystal glass, 134
Erie Train Boy (Alger), 115
Errand Boy (Alger), 115
Ethelswith, Queen of Mercia, 162
Evangeline (Longfellow), 85

Fabergé, 16-19, 187
Fabergé Easter eggs, 16-19
Fabrics, 160
Feast of the Roses, 135-136
Federal Bureau of Investigation, 95
Fenders, 100
Feodorovna, Alexandra, 17, 18
Feodorovna, Marie, 17, 19
Field, James C., 181
Fielding, William J., 25
Fire Association of Philadelphia, 154

Fire engines, 77
Fire Insurance Company of
    New Orleans, 155
Firemen's Insurance Company
    of Baltimore, 156
Firemen's Insurance Company
    of 'the District of
    Columbia, 156
Firemen's Insurance Company
    of Pittsburgh, 156
Fisher, Kate, 79
$500 (Alger), 115
Fonotipia (phonograph
    record), 185
Ford, Bob, 79, 93
Fort McHenry, 48
Fouquet, 94
Franklin, Benjamin, 10, 27,
    28, 117, 144, 145
Franklin Insurance Company,
    St. Louis, 156
Frederick II, 34
Fremont, John C., 182
French Decca (phonograph
    record), 185
Freud, Sigmund, 29
Frietchie, Barbara, 28

Gardner, Ralph, 114, 115
Gems, 33-38, 146, 147,
    175-179
    Cullinan diamond, 33-34
    Kohinoor diamond, 35
    Pigot diamond, 37
    Pitt diamond, 35-36
    Punch Jones diamond, 147
    royal items, 34-35
    Sancy diamond, 35
    Star of Arkansas diamond,
        147
    Stuart sapphire, 36
    Vargas diamond, 146
George Eastman House, 123,
    124

George III, 36
Geronimo's Story (Barrett), 81
Gettysburg Address, 23, 26
Ghia of Turin, 195
Glass Menagerie, The
    (Williams), 116
Glassboro Paint, 131
Glenn, John, 27
Gliddens, Charles, 80
Goblets, 164
Godey's (magazine), 120
Godfrey, Arthur, 8
Gold, 176
Gold powder, 162
Golden Argosy (magazine),
    120
Golden Book of Venice, 118
Goldsmith's Hall, 167
Gomm, Lady, 172
Good, Sarah, 99
Graham, Barbara, 95
Granger, Mrs., 36
Grant, Gordon, 193
Graupner, Johann Christian
    Gottlieb, 50
Great Kazan Cathedral, 188,
    189
Grebe radio, 183
Greco, El, 65
Greeley, Horace, 182
Guarnieri, Giuseppe Antonio,
    47
Gump's Department Store, 89
Gurney, Goldsworthy, 75

Hairwork jewelry, 163
Haish, Jacob, 80
Hamilton, see Alger, Horatio
Hamlet (Shakespeare), 113,
    116
Hancock, John, 27
Hancock, Walter, 75
Hancock, Winfield S., 182
Harding, W. C., 139

Harman, S. W., 81
Harper's Magazine, 189
Harrah's Collection (cars), 76
Hartford County Mutual Fire
    Insurance Company, 156
Hathaway, Anne, 163
Hauser, Kasper, 93-94
Hell on the Border (Harman),
    81
Helm, Mrs. Mary S., 81
Hemingway, Ernest, 116
Henry, O., 67
Henry II, 55
Henry VIII, 35
Henry Ford Museum, 75
Hepplewhite furniture, 142
Herbert, Victor, 48
Hex signs, 55-56
Hickock, Wild Bill, 79
Hind, Arthur, 171
Hitching posts, 128
Hitler, Adolph, 93
Hokusai, Katsushika, 65
Holbein, Hans, 35
Holliday, Doc, 79
Holy Grail, 71-73
Holy Shroud, 7, 39, 44
Home Insurance
    Company, 157
Hope, Bob, 184
Hope Mutual Insurance
    Company of
    Philadelphia, 155
Hopkinson, Francis, 49, 50
Horn of Plenty dishes, 133
Hornbooks, 101
House of Savoy (Turin), 41
Howe, Elizabeth, 99
Huber's Museum, 22
Hughes, Charles E., 182
Hunter, William, 134
Huntington, Samuel, 28

Icons, 187-190

Idle, Hermann, 11
Ignatius, St., 53
Inness, George, 83-84
Inquisition, 97
Insurance Company of
    Florida, 157
Insurance Company of
    North America, 152-154
International Zonophone
    Company, 185
Ives, James Merritt, 121-124
Ives, Joseph, 140

Jack the Ripper, 96-97
Jackson, Andy, 67
Jacobs, George, Sr., 99
Jade, 177-178
Jadeite, 177-178
James, Frank, 79
James, Jesse, 80, 93
James, W. H., 75
James II, 34, 35, 36
Jarvis, Deming, 132-133
Jesus Christ, 72
Joe's Luck (Alger), 115
Jolson, Al, 184, 185
Jones, John Paul, 54
Joseph of Arimathea, 72
Joy, Henry, 76

Kellogg prints, 123
Kemmler, 95
Kendall, Robert, 60
Kendrotas, Theodore, 58-59
Ketch, Jack, 98
Key, Francis Scott, 48
Keys, poison, 98
King, Rufus, 182
Knoumit, Princess, 161
Koundourakis, Viannis, 58
Kurz, 123
Kyritsis, Mathon, 58-60

Lace glass, 131

Laclede Mutual Insurance
    Company, 156
Lad and Lion (Burroughs),
    116
Ladder-back high chairs, 100
LaFayette, Marquis de, 98
LaFollette, Robert M., 182
Lamb, Charles, 118
Lamb, Mary, 118
Landolfi, Carlo, 12
Landon, Alfred, 182
Lauder, Harry, 185
Laurentian Library, 36
Legends
    ghost of the blue dog, 7
    golden horseshoes,
        109-111
Letters, 27-32
    Danton, Georges
        Jacques, 28
    Darwin, Charles, 29
    Dickens, Charles, 117
    Franklin, Benjamin, 27
    Freud, Sigmund, 29
    Huntington, Samuel, 28
    Key, Francis Scott, 48
    Lincoln, Abraham, 20-22
    Lindbergh, Charles, 27
    Longfellow, Henry
        Wadsworth, 117
    Reik, Theodore, 29
    Shakespeare, William,
        29-30
    Shelley, Percy
        Bysshe, 30
Lewis, Meriwether, 10
Lexington (ship), 198
Liberty Bell, 51
Library of Congress,
    22, 48, 49
"Life of a Hunter—A Tight
    Fix, The" (print), 121
Lincoln, Abraham, 20-22,
    122, 125, 173
Lind, Jenny, 30

Lindbergh, Charles, 27
Lion and Arbuckle
    Coffee ads, 68
"Little Maid of Arcadee"
    (Gilbert and Sullivan),
    49
L'Obeissante (automobile),
    75
London, Jack, 67
London Plague, 55
Long Island Automobile
    Museum, 76
Longfellow, Henry
    Wadsworth, 85, 117
Lorenzo, Pier di, 63, 64
Lost Badger Mine, 196
Lost Bonanza Mine, 196
Lost Cement Mine, 196-197
Lost Pegleg Mine, 196
Louis XIV, 94
Louis XV, 159
Louis XV furniture, 142, 143
Louis XVI, 8
Louise, Queen, 17
Lowestoft china, 165
Lucignano d'Arbia Church,
    63
Luke Walton (Alger), 115
Luz, Lester A., 187
Lyon, James, 50

McClellan, George, 182
McCormack, John, 185
McCulley, 81
McDermott, Thomas, 34
MacDonald, Jeanette, 184
Maceroni, 75
Mack, Connie, 192
McKearin, Helen, 134
Madame Tussaud's Chamber
    of Horrors, 98
Magazines, 119-120, 184, 185
Magee, Harry "Hap," 80
Mammoth Mine, 196-197

Man Without a Soul, The
  (Burroughs), 116
Manet, Edouard, 65
Marconi radio sets, 183
Marie Antoinette, Queen, 8
Mark Stanton (Alger), 115
Marlowe, Julia, 186
Martin, Susanna, 99
Martini, Simone, 64
Marvelous Land of Oz, The
  (Baum), 114
Mary, Queen of Scots, 93
Maryland's Great Seal, 8
Massachusetts Oak Tree coins,
  107
Massachusetts Pine Tree coins,
  107
Massachusetts Willow Tree
  coins, 107
Masterson, Bat, 79
Mauritius stamps, 171-172
Medici, Catherine de', 138
Medici, Lorenzo de', 36, 37
Medici china, 165
Mees, Charles Edward
  Kenneth, 124
Melba, Nellie, 185
Merchant of Venice, The
  (Shakespeare), 29
Merida (ship), 197
Metropolitan Museum, 72, 73
Milk glass, 134
Mill, Henry, 69
Mills, David, 23
Mitchell-Hedges, Anna, 189
Mkwawa's skull, 7, 51-52
Mobile Fire Department
  Insurance Company, 155
Modigliani, Amedeo, 65
Monmouth, Duke of, 94
Moore, 81
Moore, Grace, 185
More, Sir Thomas, 30
Morgan, Henry de, 161

Mudd, Dr., 95
Murders in the Rue Morgue
  (Poe), 112
Museum of Science and
  Industry, 76
Musical instruments, 45-48
Musical scores, 48-50
Mutual Assurance Company
  for Insuring Houses from
  Loss by Fire, 154
Mutual Assurance Company of
  New York City, 157
Mutual Insurance Company,
  Charleston, S. C., 155
Mutual Insurance Company of
  Washington County,
  Hagerstown, Md., 156
Mysteries, clues to famous,
  93-99

Napoleon I, 28, 88, 118, 188
National Gallery of Art, 83
National Geographic
  (magazine), 120
National Geographic Society, 8
National Society of Interior
  Designers, 9
Necklaces, 161
Ned Newton (Alger), 115
Nephrite, 177-178
Nepton, 81
New Wonderland, A (Baum),
  114
New York Boy (Alger), 115
New York Weekly
  (magazine), 120
Newgate Prison, 98
Newspapers, 117
Niagara District Mutual Fire
  Insurance Company, 157
Niccoli, Niccolo de', 36
Nicholas II, 17, 18
Niepce, Joseph Nicé Phore,
  124
Normandy, Duke of, 109

Norseman (automobile), 195-196
North Electric Company, 183
Nourse, Rebecca, 99

Odéon (phonograph record), 185
Ogle, 75
Old Crow Distillery Company, 67
Old Crow Historical Bureau, 67
Old Dartmouth Historical Society and Whaling Museum, 85
Oregon Trail, 82
Our Lady of Kazan Shrine, 189
Outdoor Life (magazine), 120
Outlaws, The (Armstrong), 81
Over the Santa Fe Trail (Nepton), 81
Overland with Kit Carson (Brewerton), 81
Owens Bottle Company, 132

Packard automobile (1901), 76-77
Paine, Thomas, 118
Paintings, 61-66
  lost works of American artists, 83-87
Palmer, C. A., 153
"Panorama of the Mississippi, The" (Banvard), 84-85
"Panorama of a Whaling Voyage Around the World, The" (Russell), 85
Papier mâché furniture, 143
Parke-Bernet Galleries, 9, 48
Parker, Alice, 99
Parker, Alton B., 182
Parker, Mary, 99
Passa, Frank, 12

Pathé Sapphire Bell (phonograph record), 185
Paul, Jan, 47
Paul the Peddler (Alger), 115
Pavlosich, Dmitri, 187
Peabody Fire and Marine Insurance Company, 157
Peach Bloom glass, 133
Peale, Charles Willson, 86-87
Pearcey, Mrs., 95
Pearls, 176
Penn Fire Insurance Company of Pittsburgh, 156
Penny Dreadfuls, 117
Perez, Antonio, 29
Perfume cones, 159
Peter the Great, 189
Peter Thompson (outfit), 138
Peterson's (magazine), 120
Phantom Radio Receptor, 183
Phelps, George D., 83
Philadelphia Contributionship, 154
Philippa, Queen, 37
Phonograph records, 184-185
Photographs, 121-125
Phyfe, Duncan, 144
Pia, Secondo, 29-40, 42
Pianos, 14-15
Picasso, Pablo, 65
Pierce, William, 117
Pilgrim Hall, 100
Pinckney, Charles, 182
"Pirates of Penzance, The" (Gilbert and Sullivan), 49
Pissaro, Camille, 66
Porter, Mrs. Lavinia H., 81
Portland Vase, 130
Potty chairs, 100
Prince Ananias (Herbert), 48-49

Princess Minnehaha (wooden Indian), 127
Prints, 13, 121-125
  Currier and Ives, 121-123
  Kellogg, 123
  Kurz and Allison, 123
Proctor, John, 99
Protection Fire Insurance Company, 157
Protection Mutual Fire Insurance Company, 157
Provincial furniture, 142
Provisional stamps, 168-174
Pudeator, Ann, 99
Punch Jones diamond, 147
"Puritans Going to Church, The" (Boughton), 64
Purrington, Caleb, 85
Putnam, *see* Alger, Horatio
Puzzles, 193-194

QST Magazine, 184
Quantrill, William, 80
Queen Anne furniture, 143

Race Track Tout (wooden figure), 128
Radford, C. A. Raleigh, 55
Radio tubes, 183
Radiola (radio set), 183
Radios, 183-184
Raleigh, Sir Walter, 28, 53
Ralph Raymond's Heir (Alger), 115
Rangeland Justice (McCulley), 81
Reals, Mrs. William H., 138
Red Book (magazine), 120
Red-flag law, 75
Reed, Isaac, 24
Reed, Wilmot, 99
Regan, J. H., 173
Regency furniture, 143
Reik, Theodore, 29

Relics
  of Bulle, 98
  of famous dead, 51-56
  Roman Catholicism and, 52-53
Reliquaries, 88-89
Rembrandt, 65, 123
Remington prints, 13
Renoir, Pierre Auguste, 66
Restoration Institute, 64
Retablo, 91-92
"Return of the Mayflower, The" (Boughton), 64
Revere, Paul, 164
Richard, Earl of Arundel, 37
Richard II, 53
Richards, Thomas, 193
Ridings, Sam P., 81
Ringo, Johnny, 80
Rings, 162-163
Ritter, Tex, 184
Robert Coverdale's Struggle (Alger), 115
Robert the Magnificent, 109-110
Robinson, Enoch, 132
Rogers, Billy Bowlegs, 197
Rommel, Erwin, 14
Roosevelt, Franklin D., 170-171, 181
Roosevelt, Theodore, 125
Roper, Sylvester H., 75
Rothschild, Baron, 9
Rubens, Peter Paul, 65
Rubies, 178
Russell, Benjamin, 85
Russell, Charles, 82
Russell, J. Scott, 75

S barbed wire, 80
St. Margaret's Churchyard, Westminster, 53
Salem witch trials, 28-29
Salinger, J. D., 9

Salvation Army, 10
San Benitos, 97
San Francisco Chronicle
    (Newspaper), 9
Sandwich glass, 131-132
Sandwich star compotes, 133
Sanson, Clement Henri, 98
Santa Fe Trail, 82
Santa Margarita (ship),
    197-198
Sapphires, 178-179
Sargent, John Singer, 9
Saunders, Richard *see*
    Franklin, Benjamin
Schneider, Johann, 95
School books, 101
Schouler, William, 21
Scott, J. Russell, 75
Scott, Margaret, 99
Scott, Sir Walter, 37
Scott, Winfield, 182
Scottish Crown, 36
Scottish Sword of State, 36
Scraps of Early Texas History
    (Helm), 81
Scuola Internazionale di
    Liuteria, 46
Sears Roebuck Company, 183
Seeking His Fortune (Alger),
    115
Seymour, Horatio, 182
Shakespeare, William, 7,
    29-30, 163
Sheet music, 184
Shelley, Percy Bysshe, 30
Sheppard, John C., 131
Sheraton furniture, 141
Ship Captain (wooden figure),
    128
Siena Pianoforte, 14-15
Silas Snobden's Office Boy
    (Alger), 115
Silver, 164-167
Sisler, 66

Smith, Alfred E., 182
Smith, Pegleg, 196
Smithsonian Institute, 76
Society for the Preservation of
    the Wooden Indian, 127
Spoons, 164-167
Sports mementoes, 191-194
    baseball, 191-192
    football, 192
    golf, 192-193
    items desired, 194
Squire, 75
Staffordshire china, 165
Stained-glass windows, 90-91
Stamps, 168-174
Star of Arkansas diamond, 147
Star Spangled Banner (Key),
    48
Stevens, V. G., 180, 181
Stiegel, Heinrich Wilhelm,
    135-136
Stiegel glass, 134-135
Stockholm (liner), 195
Stradivari, Antonio, 13, 45
Stradivari, Francesco, 13
Stradivarius violins, 11-13,
    45-46
Strawn, Clyde, 127
Studebaker-Packard
    Corporation, 76
Styluses, 184
Sullivan, J. J., 192
Summers, 75
Swiss Cantonal stamps, 172

Talbot, William
    Henry Fox, 124
Tarzan of the Apes
    (Burroughs), 116
Tatarakis, John, 59
Tea caddies, 165
Telephones, 182-183
Television sets, 183
Temple of Solomon, 14

Terry, Eli, 139
Terry, Silas B., 139
Theatrical items, 185-186
Thespis (Gilbert and
    Sullivan), 49
Thompson, Edward, 197
Thorne, Jim, 60
Three-footed cooking pots,
    165
Thumbprint punch bowls, 133
Thurmond, J. Strom, 182
Tiffany and Company, 25, 89
Tilden, Samuel J., 182
Timothy Crump's Ward
    (Alger), 115
Titus Andronicus
    (Shakespeare), 112
Tobin, 22
Toby jugs, 165
Tom the Bootblack
    (Alger), 115
Tom Thatcher's Fortune
    (Alger), 115
Tom Tracy (Alger), 115
Topaz, 175
Tower of London, 35
Town and Country
    (magazine), 120
Toys, 101-102
Trading cards, 102
Turin, Cathedral of, 39
Tutankhamen, 38
Twain, Mark, 118

Underwood Deviled Ham
    ads, 68
Union Insurance Company,
    Charleston, S. C., 155
United Firemen's Insurance
    Company of
    Philadelphia, 155
United States Department
    of the Interior, 176
United States Government
    Printing Office, 177

United States Insurance
    Company of Baltimore,
    Md., 155
United States National
    Museum, 75
United States Naval
    Academy, 54
United States Television
    Projection, 183
University of Upsala, 103

Van Gogh, Vincent, 65, 123
Vanity Fair (magazine), 120
Vargas diamond, 146
Venetian glass, 130-131
Venus de Milo (statue), 7
Verne, Jules, 118
Versailles Treaty, 52
Victor (phonograph record),
    48, 185
Victoria, Queen, 24
Vinci, Leonardo da, 123
Violins, 11-13
    guarnerius, 47
    methods of
        authenticating value,
        46
    Stradivarius, 11-13,
        45-46
Vogue (magazine), 120
Von Lettow, Paul, 52

Wahehe tribe, 51
Wall paper, 9
Wardell, Samuel, 99
Washington, George, 7,
    23, 29, 98, 122
Washington, Martha, 122
Washington Mutual
    Insurance Company, 157
Watches, 137-140
Waterford crystal, 134
Weaver, James, 181, 182
Webster, Daniel, 68
Wells, Frederick, 33

Western Boy, The
    (Alger), 115
Western Mutual Fire and
    Marine Insurance
    Company, 156
Whitelock, M. C., 11
Whiteman, Gid, 196
Whitney, Ebenezer, 132
Whittier, John Greenleaf, 28
Wilds, Sarah, 99
Wilkie, Wendell, 182
Willard, Aaron, 139
Willard, Aaron Jr., 139
Willard, John, 99
Willard, Simon, 139
William the Conqueror, 109
Winton, Alexander, 77

Wistar, Caspar, 131-132
Wistar glass, 131-132
Witchcraft relics, 98-99
*Wonderful Wizard of Oz,
    The* (Baum), 114
Worcester china, 165-166
Wren Winter's Triumph
    (Alger), 115
Wurlitzer, 13

Yanovsky, Mathis, 14
Young Outlaw (Alger), 115
Younger, Cole, 80
Younger, Jim, 80

Zer, Queen of, 162